Communicating with Children from Birth to Four Years

Communicating with Children from Birth to Four Years is an encouraging guide for practitioners and students working with young children in the Early Years Foundation Stage. The book will also appeal to parents and family carers. Providing a clear outline of children's needs, responses and abilities at each developmental stage, it guides the reader on:

- how to recognise and predict children's individual feelings and reactions;
- how to talk and listen to children at different stages;
- how to be aware of body language and other non-verbal forms of communication;
- how to support communication for children with special and additional needs.

Offering advice, ideas and strategies for supporting relationships and understanding in diverse settings and at home, this book is an essential guide to developing communication and social skills in the early years.

Debbie Chalmers is an early years practitioner, a drama teacher and consultant, and a freelance early years and primary education writer.

Communicating with Children from Birth to Four Years

Debbie Chalmers

Routledge
Taylor & Francis Group
LONDON AND NEW YORK

First published 2017
by Routledge
2 Park Square, Milton Park, Abingdon, Oxon OX14 4RN

and by Routledge
711 Third Avenue, New York, NY 10017

Routledge is an imprint of the Taylor & Francis Group, an informa business

© 2017 Debbie Chalmers

The right of Debbie Chalmers to be identified as author of this work has been asserted by her in accordance with sections 77 and 78 of the Copyright, Designs and Patents Act 1988.

All rights reserved. No part of this book may be reprinted or reproduced or utilised in any form or by any electronic, mechanical, or other means, now known or hereafter invented, including photocopying and recording, or in any information storage or retrieval system, without permission in writing from the publishers.

Trademark notice: Product or corporate names may be trademarks or registered trademarks, and are used only for identification and explanation without intent to infringe.

British Library Cataloguing in Publication Data
A catalogue record for this book is available from the British Library

Library of Congress Cataloging in Publication Data
Names: Chalmers, Debbie, 1966- author.
Title: Communicating with children from birth to four years / Debbie Chalmers.
Description: Abingdon, Oxon ; New York : Routledge is an imprint of the Taylor & Francis Group, an Informa Business, [2017]
Identifiers: LCCN 2016002130| ISBN 9781138917248 (hardback) | ISBN 9781138917255 (pbk.) | ISBN 9781315689142 (ebook)
Subjects: LCSH: Interpersonal communication in children. | Nonverbal communication in children. | Interpersonal communication in infants. | Nonverbal communication in infants. | Children and adults.Classification: LCC BF723.C57 C45 2017 | DDC 155.42/236–dc23LC
record available at http://lccn.loc.gov/2016002130

ISBN: 978-1-138-91724-8 (hbk)
ISBN: 978-1-138-91725-5 (pbk)
ISBN: 978-1-315-68914-2 (ebk)

Typeset in Zapf Humanist
by Cenveo Publisher Services

Contents

Introduction	vii
1 Starting at the beginning: birth to six months	1
2 Taking notice: six months to twelve months	10
3 Developing personality: twelve months to eighteen months	21
4 Branching out: eighteen months to twenty-four months	36
5 Fighting for independence: two years to two and a half years	48
6 Enlarging the social circle: two and a half years to three years	63
7 Finding a place: three years to three and a half years	83
8 Letting creativity soar: three and a half years to four years	103
Bibliography	122
Index	124

Introduction

The ability to communicate with others within our world is vital. Although we may automatically imagine speaking and listening or reading and writing when we think about communication, there are also many other ways to make our ideas, opinions, feelings and needs known.

Babies communicate quite effectively through crying and, as they grow, children use a variety of non-verbal methods, including sounds, gestures and pointing, to make their wishes clear. In adulthood, body language continues to play its part in communicating feelings, emotions and empathy. Many people speak more than one language, or supplement mimes or gestures for some words, particularly when using a less familiar language. Others communicate by using a recognised sign language.

Social skills are enhanced and frustrations reduced by our ability to communicate and we may often be judged by the clarity of our speech or signing and the speed of our understanding. The ability to speak and read fluently and to write clearly and correctly is a great asset throughout life and crucial for success in some jobs and careers. Creativity within speaking and writing and the ability to tell a good story may be much admired and turned into a lucrative career path.

But do we all learn to communicate inevitably and by lucky accident? Research has shown, and parents and those who work with young children know, that the greatest developments occur within the first four years of a child's life. The ability to speak, listen and understand fluently and the early stages of reading and writing are all embedded during this time. If a child receives adequate stimulation and is rewarded for his attempts to communicate with the care and attention he desires from his earliest days, he will progress to become an independent four year old, with his own ideas, opinions

Introduction

and reasoning skills, who is confident enough to speak to other children and adults and able to communicate his own wishes, take turns in conversations, discuss, negotiate, empathise and agree to differ without unbearable frustration.

This book is a practical guide for all those who live or work with young children, in which the author shares the knowledge, tips and observations she has gathered during her many years of experience as an early years practitioner and as a mother. It explains both why and how we should teach our children to develop strong communication skills and illustrates how this can help us to value and enjoy their company at every stage.

The book is divided into chapters that each cover six months of development, although all children develop at individual rates and the age ranges given are for guidance only. Adults may read the chapters in chronological order while bringing up one family, or dip in and out of the book to find ideas and advice for specific children, problems or areas of interest.

Sometimes children behave or react in unexpected ways or are unable to describe what they need. At various times they may not have the vocabulary, the understanding or the social skills to express themselves clearly or appropriately. This can cause frustrations and undesirable behaviour that they may not have the ability to control. Adults must be prepared to see through the behaviour to the problems beneath and step in at these times to defuse situations, explain, support and restore good humour.

Children's needs, responses, reactions, feelings and attitudes change frequently as they grow from babies to toddlers and then to children. What they like one week may not interest them the next. Their favourite games and toys may change every two to three weeks, along with their routines, mealtimes and sleep patterns. Their physical needs, such as hunger, thirst, warmth and reassurance take precedence over intellectual and social considerations.

Babies and toddlers respond well to a particular type of speech, but as children grow older they prefer a different approach. Sharing games, activities, conversations, songs, rhymes and stories can strengthen relationships and enhance learning at each age and stage. Children must be encouraged to play constructively with siblings and friends and given frequent opportunities to practise, so that they may learn to speak and understand, ask questions, solve problems, observe manners and customs and empathise with others, while being offered the right guidance and support.

Some children have particular needs or specific characteristics that require different approaches and specialist support to ensure that their communication

Introduction

needs are met. Adults have a duty to seek out and provide appropriate types and levels of specialist advice and intervention when children's special needs are identified.

Parents and carers may often feel that as soon as they feel confident of what to do with their children, it stops working. Practitioners may sometimes assume that what is right for several children will be right for a whole group. The reality is that no two children are the same and their needs change continuously. The only way to keep up and to continue to provide the best care and learning experiences is to establish strong relationships based on excellent communication, to respect children as individuals and to provide a safe and secure base from which they can move out into the world when the time is right and to which they can return whenever they choose.

When adults know their children intimately, they are able to react instinctively to prevent problems arising, to avert clashes and disasters or to support them in learning to handle excitement, disappointment and other strong emotions. Knowing how to speak to children and when to speak on their behalf brings confidence and satisfaction to the relationships that adults form with them.

This book details the situations in which children need or want to communicate with adults and with each other, from the time of birth to the age of four years. It is illustrated throughout with photographs and case studies that bring the advice to life and prove its relevance to the real world in which we live today.

Our greatest speakers, writers, actors and leaders of the country had to develop their communication skills during their foundation years, before they were five years old. They did so with the help of interested and nurturing families and skilled and experienced childcare and education professionals. We must all be mindful of the fact that young children need our help, support and guidance as they learn to communicate effectively, and that any of the children we care for or work with today may be a huge influence upon the world tomorrow.

Starting at the beginning
Birth to six months

From birth tiny babies communicate with their primary caregivers, whether parents, grandparents, nannies or other guardians. In waking moments they seek out a familiar human face for stimulation, comfort and security. Their little faces may be consumed by earnest expressions, which are a mixture of concentration and wonder. This shows us that their brains are absorbing information rapidly to allow their minds and bodies to develop, and it reminds us that another precious new life has just begun.

They will copy expressions such as frowns, closed eyes, wrinkled noses and tongues poking out and may move their mouths in attempts to mimic the movements of adults who are speaking to them. They may copy the smiles that are directed at them. These are not yet deliberate smiles to communicate happiness or serve as a greeting, but they are instinctive first attempts to please adults, to hold their attention and to make them want to continue the interactions.

> Verity, aged two weeks, enjoys being held and talked to by a caring adult. She can only focus on a face that is close to hers, but concentrates hard to do so, moving her face and mouth in an attempt to mimic the expressions and sounds that she is hearing. The more the adult smiles and speaks to her, the more she tries to respond. This is rewarding for both of them, so they seek to continue the interaction until Verity becomes tired.

Birth to six months

From the very beginning of babies' lives, it is important that primary caregivers sing songs and lullabies and rock in time with the rhythms. This develops feelings of security and a sense of balance, as well as a strong emotional bond between adults and children. As babies grow older, hearing voices singing helps them to pay attention to rhythms and sounds within words, which prepares them for language development later on.

Early interactions

Between four and six weeks, a baby will begin to smile deliberately, having already learned that this attracts or maintains attention and brings the reward of satisfying and pleasurable interactions with familiar adults or older siblings. Family members and those who choose to work with babies respond to the small advances they make and so teach them the art of giving and taking turns in conversation from the very beginning. As it will be many months before they can communicate verbally, babies rely on body language and respond with expressions and actions when stimulated by their carers.

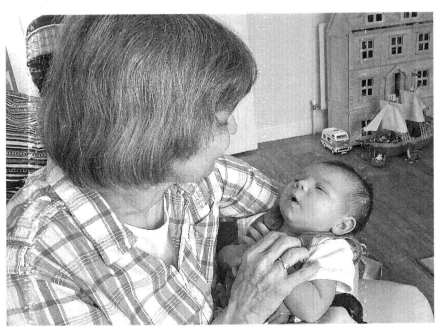

Figure 1.1 Young babies form strong emotional bonds with adults who speak and sing to them.

Birth to six months

Babies will now be able to make and maintain eye contact with familiar people who choose to continue this with them, and they will have enough control of their eye movements to follow carers as they approach or pass by, although their range of vision is still very limited and they will only see a face clearly when it is close to them. They may begin to reach out to touch faces and will take pleasure in their hands being held or stroked.

> Lucy, aged two months, watches adults and older children intently as they approach her and moves her head to follow them. When they speak to her she makes eye contact and smiles and wriggles, which makes them more likely to speak to her again. When fully engaged in this type of interaction, Lucy makes noises of her own that mimic the sounds of words heard indistinctly, as if from a conversation a short distance away. Already, her brain is beginning to formulate the general sounds and the give and take nature of human speech.

Small babies use crying as a main form of communication. Their carers respond to the cries and seek to satisfy the babies' needs, deciding whether they are hungry or thirsty, too hot or too cold, uncomfortable, unwell, bored,

Figure 1.2 Babies are soothed by carers who hold them closely and talk to them confidently.

lonely, over- or under-stimulated or just tired. A confident adult or older child may soothe a baby with their presence, by holding, rocking or stroking or by speaking or singing.

The use of 'parentese' language, in which words are simplified, repeated and exaggerated and a higher pitched tone of voice is used, attracts and holds the attention of the baby. Before the age of five or six months, most babies are fairly happy to be soothed and distracted by any appropriate and available caring adult and will seek to gain the attention of those around them.

> Elliott, aged four months, is asked by his father, 'Would you like a drink now? Are you ready for your milk?' as he holds up his bottle. Elliott sees and smells the warm milk and wriggles a little in his arms in anticipation. Before the bottle touches his mouth he is already making a sucking motion with his lips and, as he begins to drink the milk, he closes his eyes for a moment and then opens them to gaze fixedly at his father's face.
>
> After a short time Elliott stops sucking and makes some small cries of discomfort. His father removes the bottle from his mouth and sits him up on his lap to rub his back. After a few moments, Elliott stops wriggling and crying and opens his mouth again. His father takes him back into his arms and replaces the bottle in his mouth and he sucks happily.

Personal care routines

A baby's desire to communicate is stimulated by feelings of comfort and pleasure. First attempts to establish close contacts will develop during feeding times, provided caring adults take time to hold babies close and maintain eye contact, while gently encouraging sucking and allowing them to take as much milk as they need and to enjoy it at their own pace.

When parents, siblings, other family members, friends or professional carers spend time feeding the same babies regularly, they become aware of their feelings and alert to their signals. Small wriggles of pleasure are recognised as different from squirms of discomfort and carers will know when to adjust

Birth to six months

Figure 1.3 Feeding babies regularly allows carers to become attuned to their feelings and signals.

a baby's position or temporarily stop feeding and attempt to bring up the baby's wind. They will also know when to gently encourage a sleepy baby to take a little more milk towards the end of a feed and when to stop feeding because the baby is uncomfortable, unhappy or full. This type of communication is instinctive and happens naturally. Both baby and carer read each other's signals and feel relaxed and confident in each other's company.

If instinctive communication is missing, because a baby's needs are not recognised by a caring adult or regular care and attention is lacking in a baby's life, the ability to form strong bonds and attachments is adversely affected. The child is likely to have difficulty with relationships in the early years and beyond unless the situation is rectified in time. Without strong, secure relationships, consistent loving care and attention and adequate and appropriate stimulation, the development of communication skills will be delayed or may not follow the expected pattern.

Young babies like to hear familiar sounds and family noise around them because they are soothing and comforting. Silence can be frightening, especially if it comes too suddenly. While babies do need a quiet place to sleep, and should begin to learn quickly the difference between night and day using a lack of noise and light as clues, they will sleep when they are tired and are happy to drop off while being held or carried, or in a pram, cot or basket in the corner of a family room or nursery. They will also sleep in a car, pushchair or sling while the rest of their family or their carers go about essential business.

Birth to six months

Putting small babies into a separate room some distance away from the group, and asking everybody to be silent while they sleep, can send a message to the baby that they are not wanted at that time and they must miss out on whatever is going on. Keeping them close and expecting them to sleep despite normal sounds and a low level of noise during the day communicates that they are still a part of the group and that they will be welcomed back as soon as they wake. A greater sense of security comes from the feeling that they are not alone and their needs will still be met as soon as they make them known. This can make them less likely to wake before they have slept enough and calm rather than fretful.

From a young age babies develop different types of cries to fit different situations. For example, the screaming in pain, the noisy cries of hunger and the fretful grizzling of tiredness are easily distinguishable and recognised by regular caregivers. This enables them to distinguish between more urgent needs that must be satisfied, with a feed, a nappy change or a change of position, and general discomfort, which may be relieved by the distraction of a toy, a song, or a change of scene.

Gradually, as babies grow older, they use different sounds as well as crying, and begin to take turns in early conversations, listening to speech and then making some similar sounds in response, both while they are being spoken to and in any gaps left between sentences.

Different sounds and languages

Babies have to learn sounds before they can reproduce them. From their earliest months of life, babies can recognise certain familiar voices, distinguish between languages and show a preference for their mothers' voices and the languages the mothers used while they were in the womb. They are born with experience in learning these languages, as the pitch, rhythm and sounds of the speech are already familiar to them.

Infants who use two or more languages with adults from their earliest days instinctively understand that they follow separate rules, systems and formats and effortlessly keep them apart and distinguish between them without conscious thought. Being multilingual from birth does not interfere with children's development in any way and they are expected to meet milestones at the same ages and stages as those who are monolingual.

Adults living and working with children should understand and remember that more than 70 per cent of the population of the world is bilingual and these people use two languages daily in their normal lives. Many use more than two languages and it is, in fact, a minority of people who speak and understand only one language. However, those who use a single language usually speak one that is widely used and understood throughout the world, such as English. When people travel to a new country to live, stay or work, they need to learn to understand and express themselves in the dominant language of that culture, while retaining their own first languages and their linguistic identity.

> Bian, aged six months, is in her pushchair at the station with her brother, Arun, aged 17 months. Their mother is buying tickets for a future journey from the machine. Bian looks at Arun's face until he looks at her and smiles. She smiles back at him. He then makes a funny face at her, waving his head from side to side. She copies this expression and head movement too.
>
> Arun then looks away and begins to fidget in the pushchair, so Bian looks at her mother instead, smiling and waving her arms, but her mother does not notice. Bian makes sounds to attract her mother's attention, but she is concentrating on the ticket machine and cannot look at the baby. Bian switches her attention back to her brother and makes sounds while looking at his face. Arun copies the sounds and then claps his hands. Bian lifts her arms again and almost brings her hands together to clap.

Babies crave attention from family members and familiar caregivers and enjoy interactions involving facial expressions, movements and sounds. When their basic needs are satisfied and they are looking only for entertainment, they are able to work out for themselves who is most likely to respond to them and are as happy to play with an older child as with an adult.

Stimulation and play

All humans are more likely to talk if they have something interesting to talk about and very young babies are no exception. Although they cannot yet use recognisable speech, they will vocalise as though making attempts at words if

Birth to six months

Figure 1.4 Babies enjoy copying and sharing facial expressions with family members.

they are stimulated. Bright toys and objects in interesting shapes, their movements and the shadows they cast, the sounds they make and the textures they have if touched can stimulate babies to want to speak and encourage them to make sounds to express their feelings of excitement and to attract the attention of those around them. The desire to tell others of what they have discovered is an instinct that will stay with them throughout their lives.

Providing a safe place to lie and look up at toys suspended from a frame can offer valuable stimulation and free movement for young babies and will encourage them to vocalise. If some of the toys make sounds when touched they may attempt to make sounds in return, thus taking first steps towards an understanding of turn taking and keeping a conversation or communication going.

Although many commercially produced 'baby gyms' are available for purchase, toys and objects may be also hung on strings from any suitable surface under which babies can safely lie. Equipment such as this can be very convenient when there is sufficient space and especially where there are several babies to use it, such as in a nursery or a childminder's setting, but parents should choose whether they would prefer to create a similar environment of

Birth to six months

Figure 1.5 Hanging toys can create a safe and stimulating environment in which babies can play.

their own, especially when space is more limited. Whether using a frame or not, it is important to select toys and other objects that are likely to hold the babies' interest and to add to them and change them regularly.

Such an activity can provide a safe place for babies, with comfort and stimulation for short periods while adults carry out other essential tasks, but it is also very valuable to sit beside the babies as they play and touch and talk about the toys and objects they can see. Babies are more likely to continue with their exploration of objects, reach out to toys and make sounds if their efforts are rewarded by praise and encouragement from carers. They will welcome more new opportunities to play and develop if they associate the activity with reassurance and enjoyment, but will resist being placed on the mat or cry and reject the toys offered if they know that they are always left alone there and cannot understand how to play by themselves.

By the age of six months most babies will be sitting unaided or with a little support and reaching out for the people, toys and objects that they want. They will begin to point to things and make sounds. Their parents and carers may look at what interests the babies and talk about what they can see, or pass the desired objects to them and name them. In this way, the babies collect vocabulary that they will later use to fetch or ask for the items that they need.

Taking notice
Six months to twelve months

Parents and carers will always be advised that it is vitally important to help children to learn to understand and use speech from a very early age. Some research has shown that the number of words known and used by toddlers can predict how easily and confidently they will learn to speak, listen and read by school age.

Words, names and labels

Children can more easily learn and remember names if adults say the words clearly while focusing attention on the relevant people, pets and objects. Showing a child a specific item or pointing to it in a picture or photograph while saying its name, or looking at a particular person or animal while talking to or about them and using the correct name, helps the child to learn the words and label things correctly.

From six to twelve months, babies continue to point to people, items and pictures and to make sounds. They may use a particular sound while pointing, which their parents and carers interpret as 'What's that?' or 'I want that'. If adults say 'Yes, look at that' or 'Would you like this?' and go on to name the items, the babies will learn to use these phrases for themselves and also gradually absorb the names of the things they want to talk about. They will also understand common questions, ideas and instructions and may indicate their responses through their body language.

As their range and clearness of vision increases gradually, they will watch people intently, seeking out human faces of strangers as well as carers, and continue to practise expressions by copying what they see around them.

Six months to twelve months

> Harriet, aged eight months, is in the supermarket with her uncle. She watches as her uncle picks up items from the shelves and looks behind her as they are placed into the trolley under her seat. Whenever her uncle looks at her, she smiles at him, and when he says, 'Good girl, Harriet!' she claps her hands.
>
> He walks away from the trolley to fetch another item from a display, looking back at her and waving his hand. Harriet waves her hands and watches him anxiously, bouncing with pleasure when he returns to her. Soon he says, 'Do you want to come out?' and holds out his arms. Harriet holds out her arms and bounces in her seat again until her uncle unfastens her straps and lifts her out for a cuddle.

Older babies recognise their own names if they are used often enough, and also familiar people and their voices, turning when they see and hear them and expressing pleasure through happy and excited sounds, facial expressions and movements. They are keen to hold conversations and understand the concept of turn taking through speaking and then listening. They may express sounds and first words in more than one language and may still rely on gestures to communicate their meanings at times, or use recognised signs.

Adults should aim to use babies' names as often as possible and watch carefully to ensure that they are responding to them, to prove that their development is progressing satisfactorily, both in hearing and understanding.

> Holly, aged nine months, turns to the speaker if she hears her name or recognises a familiar voice. She initiates conversations by pointing at objects or holding out toys while making sounds and is rewarded when somebody replies to her with the name of the object she is indicating or a sentence about what she can see or what she is doing.
>
> She enjoys looking at books and listening to music with her older sister and makes babbling sounds to join in with the reading and singing. If her sister points to a picture and says 'Look, it's a cat', Holly points to it too and makes a sound a little like 'cat'. Their mother then reinforces the communication between the two girls and stimulates their further understanding by saying, 'You can see a cat in the book and it has a long tail'.

Six months to twelve months

Figure 2.1 Babies must learn to take turns to speak and to listen in preparation for later conversations.

Very first words, that a baby uses deliberately and repeatedly to express a particular meaning, are often repeated sounds such as 'Mama' or 'Dada'. Primary caregivers may also recognise repeated collections of sounds that are a baby's attempts to say certain words or phrases, although the separate words are not clearly formed. Simple phrases, such as 'all gone' and 'oh dear', are common examples. Adults should praise babies for all attempts at speech and understanding and reward them with attention and affection, while repeating what they wanted to say and supplying the correct words or longer phrases and sentences to stimulate further development.

Languages, sounds and phrases

During the first months of life, all babies make similar sounds but, from about nine months, they begin to focus on the sounds in the language(s) they hear regularly and stop using those that are not spoken around them.

All babies, all over the world, first babble with vowel sounds and a few consonants such as 'd' and 'm'. The sequence in which sounds are mastered is linked to the development of babies' tongues and mouth muscles and the emergence of teeth. The more complex sounds 'r' and 'y' are usually the last ones that English-speaking children master.

Although all babies begin to babble using a full range of sounds, they quickly recognise and continue to make the ones that occur in their first languages and stop making those which they do not hear. When babies from different cultures regularly spend time together they will all make sounds that occur in the language spoken within the setting, but those from other cultures, with other home languages, will also make sounds that they hear within their own families. This will enable them to go on to become bilingual once they learn to speak.

It is important for carers to reward all babies' attempts to communicate with smiles and responses, but these need not be in the babies' first languages. Children will learn to speak two languages easily if they communicate in one language in their early years setting and another with certain family members at home. Practitioners should simply celebrate all children as individuals and respect their different languages, accents and ways of speaking and understanding.

Some babies use dummies for comfort and to help them to fall asleep. While there is some evidence that these can help to keep airways open and allow young babies to learn to suck and to breathe strongly, which has suggested a possible link with reducing the risk of sudden infant death syndrome (also known as cot death), it is unlikely that there is any further value of this kind to be gained after the age of one year. It is advisable to swap to a different type of comforter at this age and to discourage the use of dummies, or to ensure that they are only used at sleep times.

A dummy in the mouth of a child who is awake and ready to communicate can impede speech development, preventing the tongue from touching the teeth and discouraging the child from opening the mouth fully so that certain sounds cannot be formed. This can make it impossible to understand what the child is trying to say. Reliance upon a dummy during the early years can mean that a child does not bother to try to form words and sounds correctly or attempt intelligible speech, but either continues to slur and adapt sounds to accommodate the dummy in the mouth, hoping that parents and carers will work out or guess what was meant, or seldom tries to speak at all.

> In the baby room the children aged six to twelve months are gradually waking from their naps. The practitioners can hear them babbling to themselves and to each other and are ready to go to lift them from their cots. They first listen carefully to decide which babies have woken as they want to avoid disturbing those who are still sleeping.
>
> One key person listens very hard until she hears certain sounds that she associates with her key children and says, 'James is awake and talking to himself. He's making that new sound he learned yesterday. And that's Charlie just waking now, because he always grizzles and mutters for a moment before he calls out'.
>
> Another key person says, 'I can't hear Alex at all and he does usually sleep longer, so I'll just check on him on my way past. But we can all hear that Aaro is awake because none of the other babies make that sound. It's from a word that means Mummy in Finnish, isn't it? It's what he says when she arrives to collect him'.

Gestures, signs and social actions

Babies who can sit unsupported or who are mobile crawlers will have developed enough coordination of their limbs to be able to use their hands, feet, arms and legs independently and with some control. As well as hearing words and sounds and attempting to copy them, they may make gestures to communicate, such as pointing, reaching for objects, picking things up, putting things down and pushing things away.

Adults often encourage them to copy social actions, such as clapping and waving, and reward them with praise when they learn to use these appropriately. This is another form of communication that is important for humans, and babies must learn to function within their own society and culture, observing social conventions and gradually absorbing the details that tell them what they should do in polite company and what they should never do in public. As they grow older, they will learn the subtle differences between home and family behaviours, peer and friendship behaviours and stranger and formal company behaviours.

Introducing a selection of simple signs that babies can understand and sometimes use for themselves can be helpful in reducing frustration while they are struggling to develop speech. Mimes, signs and gestures can be developed for individual babies to share with familiar carers, such as putting food or drink into the mouth, putting on a hat or a sock, putting toys into a box and cuddling a doll or a teddy, and signs that mean: 'Stop', 'Come here', 'Pick it up', 'Put it down', 'Yes' and 'No'.

Instructions and repetitions

Most babies will learn to roll, crawl or shuffle between the ages of eight and twelve months and may begin to stand or walk. Their increased mobility

Figure 2.2 Pre-verbal babies can communicate through signs and gestures as well as sounds and words.

will bring them into contact with more risks and so, around this age, they will need to learn to understand and respond to the word 'No', in order to stay safe. They are able to learn that 'No' means 'Stop doing that' or 'Don't touch that' or 'Don't go over there' and may respond immediately on some occasions.

However, they will need lots of repetition and supervision and cannot yet be relied upon to respond to verbal instructions only. The word 'No' must often be accompanied by the gentle but firm removal of an object from a baby or the baby from a situation. 'Give that to me please' and 'Come here please' are other excellent phrases for babies to learn to respond to, to ensure their safety.

> Gethin, aged eleven months, plays a game with his Nanna. He passes her a toy and she takes it and says, 'Thank you!' She then passes it back and says, 'Thank you!' for him as he takes it. Gethin smiles each time she speaks and echoes her words with similar sounds. He chooses to give and take toys to continue the game until he becomes tired.

Repetitive games played with adults and older children are pleasurable for babies and provide opportunities for them to practise interactive communication and turn taking in preparation for conversation. They can also offer early experiences of using manners and social conventions, as well as building and confirming warm relationships with family members and carers.

Learning physical and gross motor skills often alternates with speech and language and fine motor skills so, once they can safely sit unsupported and reach out to play with toys and objects, babies will work on exploring with their fingers and mouths and vocalising for a while, before learning to crawl or shuffle.

Children under one year old chew toys and objects because their mouths are most sensitive to textures and they are exploring and finding out about everything they touch with their mouths as well as their fingers. They will grow their first teeth during this time and need to suck, bite and chew to help the teeth to develop and break through the gums. Babies will often dribble a lot at this time too. Mouthing hard and cold items can give them relief from the pain of teething, so providing cooled teething toys and foods and soft bibs

Six months to twelve months

Figure 2.3 Playing repetitive games with older children helps babies to learn social skills.

and face wipes will relieve their discomfort and encourage the important first teeth to come through.

New vocalisations

The existence of healthy teeth and their correct placement in the jaw are vital for speech development, as the movements of the tongue against the front teeth are essential for the formation of some sounds. Parents and carers who are tuned into their babies' vocalisations may hear new sounds being added and practised as teeth emerge.

From the age of nine months, babies are able to produce loud and sustained vocalisations. Some will squeal and shriek in high-pitched tones, in excitement, displeasure and frustration, while others will growl and grumble in lower tones, keeping up an audible hum or mutter for minutes at a time. Often they will laugh, not because something has amused them but because they are finding pleasure and satisfaction in their exploratory play. If their carers enjoy their chuckles and laugh along with them, they will learn that these sounds bring pleasure to the people who matter to them and the reward of extra attention and affection, and so they will seek to repeat these responses.

Six months to twelve months

Figure 2.4 Babies chew toys and objects to explore their textures and to help their first teeth to break through.

They will often use their voices to create an audible running commentary while absorbed in the exploration of a toy, object or texture. Although there are no distinguishable words yet, the variations, pauses and inflections of language are already present and the format of conversational speech is being developed before deliberately chosen single words. Later, the child will learn to choose and produce appropriate words and practise them separately, before putting the two concepts together to create fluent speech.

Adults should encourage this stage by responding warmly to babies' vocalisations, rewarding them with smiles and nods of agreement and offering simple descriptions of toys or activities and praise for their efforts. Babies love repetitive speech, accompanied by eye contact and physical gestures from a familiar adult or sibling, and can begin to learn the skills of conversational turn taking from this early age.

By hearing the flow of sounds, rather than listening too closely and trying to pick out individual words, adults will realise that the babies are already mastering the shape and flow of phrases and sentences, absorbing and reproducing the speech they hear around them every day and demonstrating that they are keen to talk to the people they love.

Playing together

When two or three babies sit together to play they will make different sounds at random, sometimes together and sometimes separately. However, when one baby makes a loud, sudden or sustained noise, the others are likely to respond with noises of their own. If they have frequent opportunities to play together, as in the case of twins or triplets or babies attending an early years setting, they will quickly learn to make sounds to attract each other's attention when offering or taking toys. At times they will all shout or squeal at the same time, striving to be heard in what appears to be a volume competition!

Twins and triplets often create a special form of communication between themselves, which others cannot understand. They may use a language of sounds or gestures that they develop together from a very young age and use for several years. They are also likely to be particularly empathetic and continue to understand each other's feelings and be affected by events in each other's lives, even when they are apart. In some cases, they may grow up to translate for each other, finish each other's sentences or speak alternately or in unison.

Figure 2.5 When babies play together they learn to swap and share toys and develop empathy for each other.

Sometimes one twin or triplet may be much more dominant and expect to always lead the other sibling(s) or take the greater share of adult attention, but parents and carers must always strive to ensure that the children's voices are equally heard and their wishes, feelings, reactions and opinions equally expressed and considered, thus communicating to them that each child is equally important and valued as an individual.

When a baby is upset and makes whimpering sounds or cries, other babies nearby will react by becoming unhappy or unsettled too. Those nearer to twelve months may already have developed enough empathy to try to soothe a sibling or friend by offering a toy, a comforter or a clumsy hug or kiss, especially if they are able to crawl or shuffle over to the other child. Others may cry to attract the attention of the caring adult until the upset baby receives comfort and peace is restored.

Babies often develop infectious chuckles or giggles from this stage, which delight their families and carers. Adults and older children will laugh with babies, tickle them and play peepbo games, hoping to amuse them. Their shining eyes and spontaneous laughter reward and prolong the communication and deepen and strengthen the relationships. A developing sense of humour proves that a baby is maturing in self-confidence and social skills and seeking to communicate with others and take a place in the world.

Sharing laughter and a joy in communicating with others is more important than counting the number of words a child has learned to say. A rich use of language will only develop when the desire to understand and express ideas and exchange feelings and opinions is firmly rooted in a child's personality and when constructive opportunities and experiences are freely available.

Developing personality
Twelve months to eighteen months

Young children need to be touched, for comfort, reassurance and security, and this is a powerful method of communication. Primary caregivers must have close relationships with their children to allow them to demonstrate their feelings and to understand their needs and responses. Children may be soothed to sleep, or comforted when upset or angry, in particular ways.

> Simon, aged twelve months, needs to sleep at a certain time each day or he quickly becomes over-tired, very upset and unable to cope. He is able to fall asleep quickly and, once asleep, is not easily woken until he has slept for at least an hour.
>
> One day he is out with his nanny and his three-year-old brother at an important appointment and he must sleep in the pushchair as they cannot go home in time for his sleep. Simon sits happily in the pushchair looking at books until his sleep time arrives, then he becomes fretful and can no longer sit still or be quiet. His nanny calmly takes him out to sit on her lap and strokes his back while he leans against her. When she feels him relax, she lifts him back into the pushchair and lowers it to the sleeping position, stroking his head continuously and holding his hand until he falls asleep.
>
> This process takes less than five minutes and does not prevent Simon's nanny from concentrating on his older brother or the person she is speaking to. She is undisturbed because she is completely confident that she can soothe Simon to sleep easily and the two have such a close relationship that her presence is enough to reassure Simon that he will be safe if he sleeps here.

Twelve months to eighteen months

Relationships and attachments

From this age many children will develop an attachment to a toy, blanket or other comforter and these will be important for their feelings of security and wellbeing. They may give them names that are unintelligible to anybody outside the immediate family. They may also have their own names or approximations of names for their parents, siblings, any other primary caregivers and, sometimes, for themselves.

One-year-old babies enjoy maintaining the personal attention of their parents or carers through their efforts to acquire speech and can cement their understanding of basic words and develop their memories through familiar games. For example, adults may play games such as: 'Where is your nose? Show me your eyes! Here's Mummy's mouth; can you find your mouth?' They should then point to or gently touch each body part mentioned until children begin to respond and point correctly without help.

Important vocabulary can be learned when adults use picture books containing lots of different animals, vehicles or familiar objects and encourage children to point to the correct pictures as they are named. For example, they might ask: 'Can you show me the pig? Where is the digger? Now let's find the

Figure 3.1 Sharing an adult's lap encourages siblings to bond and enjoy each other's company.

tree'. This type of varied speech sounds more natural than repeated 'Where is …?' questions and encourages more confident language learning.

Families should set aside times to share books, as reading stories and talking about pictures together encourages close relationships between parents and children and between babies and children of different ages.

Young toddlers will accept parents including babies in their activities, with no feelings of jealousy or resentment, if they share laps, books and toys from the beginning of the babies' lives. This is an example of when to choose to offer an activity that is valuable for the older child while keeping the baby safe and comfortable alongside the adult.

Carers of two or more children face a continuous juggling act and must communicate through their actions and words that their children are equally important to them and that they will always be treated fairly. Each individual's needs must be assessed in each different situation and appropriate decisions taken. There may be occasions when an older and a younger child appear to have an equal need for attention at the same time and an adult considers it sensible to attend to the child who will mind waiting before the one who will not understand. For example, a baby may be able to safely and happily wait for a few minutes before being changed into a clean outfit or nappy, while an older child first receives urgent help with a model. This will avoid the child feeling resentful of the baby because the adult was unavailable and the play was spoiled.

However, it is important that all children develop a habit of feeling and displaying consideration for others, as needs and situations will change as they grow older. So adults should ensure that, when they are already attending to the baby's needs, the older child is sometimes asked to wait until the baby is comfortable and content before expecting to receive undivided attention. Whenever possible, siblings should be invited to join in with each other's activities and to care for each other. In this way, the children will become used to sharing adult attention, taking turns, accepting compromises and playing together.

Albums of photographs are very popular with young children and allow them to practise recognising and naming important family members and friends. Some names can be difficult to pronounce, but they will find a way of producing appropriate sounds to indicate the person they mean to talk about. This can be very endearing and affectionate names of this kind often endure among families and friends for many years. There is no need to rush to correct 'pet' names as children will correct them for themselves as soon as they are able to enunciate clearly and later write them down, but they may

Twelve months to eighteen months

still choose to use the familiar sounds at times in order to feel close to the people they care about.

It is important to offer lots of praise and rewards such as smiles, cuddles and claps when babies find and point to objects or pictures spontaneously. Children should be rewarded for understanding that the adult's speech was a question to which an appropriate response was expected, and the reward may be even greater when the response is a correct one.

As children begin to attempt to imitate the speech they hear, they should be offered opportunities to name objects and pictures with single words. Praise and rewards are due when they consistently make the same sound to describe a particular picture, even if the sound is only a small part of the actual word. Vowel sounds may be used without the consonants, or the first or last syllable repeated in place of the other sounds.

> Meghan, aged fifteen months, sees a photo of her sister and points to it, looking at her mother and saying 'Oof! Oof!'
>
> Her mother replies warmly, 'Yes, that's Ruth, isn't it? You can see Ruth in the picture. That's your big sister, Ruth! Well done, Meg!'
>
> Meghan touches the picture again, smiling and saying 'Oof!' quietly to herself.

Extending vocabulary

Sometimes children deliberately draw adults' attention to what they are interested in but, at other times, adults may find it more challenging to be sure of what they are looking at and to talk about it with enthusiasm. However, it is always worth making the effort to identify and extend their interests in this way, as children will learn to understand, talk and remember much more easily and effectively while fully focused and giving their full attention to the vocabulary and speech patterns being modelled for them.

As babies begin to display an interest in learning to speak, they need to hear language from everybody around them. It is important to talk about the toys they pick up, the movements they make and the people they can see, to encourage them to respond with smiles and sounds of their own, to offer

Twelve months to eighteen months

Figure 3.2 Capture a baby's interest by talking about the toys they choose and the movements they make.

these communications as frequently as possible and to continue for as long as their interest lasts.

Protecting mouths and teeth

It is important to protect children's developing teeth and to keep their mouths and gums healthy because they are vital for clear and confident speech. Parents and carers should avoid offering sugary drinks and allowing children to suck on bottles and beaker cups between meals. Thirsty children should be offered water or milk and juice should be given only as part of a meal.

In an early years setting, practitioners will only offer milk or water to children at snack times. They will also ensure that food is healthy and balanced and appropriate to the age of the children. If parents are unsure of how to continue this at home, their child's key person should always be able and willing to advise them.

When children sit at a table or a highchair tray they should not need a lid or a spout on a cup by the age of eighteen months, but two handles may still be useful and close supervision is essential. Bedtime bottles of warm milk should be replaced with cups as soon as possible after the first birthday, although the drink and the cuddle are still a vital part of the evening routine.

Games and activities

From twelve months, babies are usually mobile and interested in everything. They will take notice of the smallest details and are very observant, making their own deductions and absorbing familiar experiences and events that happen often. From this, they gain security and self-confidence.

They may initiate games that they have often played with familiar people, such as crawling or toddling away from somebody who will pretend to chase them or peeping around a corner, then hiding and then peeping out again. This shows that these children are already trying to develop social and communication skills and all such attempts should be encouraged.

Children may demonstrate their understanding through their actions, long before they are able to verbalise what they are doing or thinking. Practising doing things to order in this way helps them to accept and thrive upon structures and routines within an organised environment later on.

> Andrew, aged seventeen months, enjoys sharing a drink with his three older siblings. His mother places four new coloured plastic cups on a tray beside them, as they sit on the floor. The three older children each choose a colour and the green cup is left, so they hand it to the baby and he happily takes it and drinks his water.
>
> Next time the children have a drink the four cups are placed on the tray again and each child takes the colour that they chose before, leaving the green cup on the tray. Andrew reaches out, takes the green cup and enjoys his drink. On future occasions he reaches out to the tray of drinks before his siblings but always takes the green cup, because he now recognises it and knows that it is his, although nobody has told him this.
>
> His mother buys some plates to match the cups and puts them out in a row with pieces of fruit on them, asking the older children to wait and see what Andrew will do. He unerringly takes the green plate and begins to eat his fruit and then is delighted that his family is pleased with him.

Twelve months to eighteen months

Figure 3.3 Games involving hiding and peeping out help to develop social and communication skills.

The development of babies' reasoning skills and memories may be encouraged, even at this pre-verbal stage, by offering them opportunities to practise. Making selections by matching colours and shapes, remembering sequences of actions and sorting objects into groups are all useful activities to work on at

Twelve months to eighteen months

Figure 3.4 Listening to conversations between adults and older children encourages toddlers to attempt to form sounds and words.

this age. There are many toys available to encourage these skills, but household objects and found items may also be used. Processes such as getting dressed, helping with the washing or food preparation and collecting objects outside in the park can also be very valuable.

Most importantly, babies need to hear adults and older children talking about what they are doing, and they need to be praised, encouraged and supported when they begin to attempt to form sounds and words to describe their own thoughts and actions.

> Peter, aged fourteen months, recognises groups and is able to sort everything into one of his groups, using a simple word or sound. Some of these are accompanied by an action or an expression to further reinforce their meaning.
>
> When he sees an animal, picks up a toy animal or points to a picture of an animal, Peter growls. In this way he is neatly placing all non-human living creatures into his animal category. So far, he does not

Twelve months to eighteen months

create any smaller groups, but growls whether he is indicating a tiger, a rabbit, a crocodile, a dinosaur, a bird or an insect. In order to attract the attention of his carers, he also makes a fierce expression, which he has learned brings the reward of laughter and affection. When he wants to speak to or about people, Peter says 'Hello', often accompanying the word with a wave of his hand. He can already instinctively sort humans from other living creatures successfully, even in pictures and small world toys.

As a banana is a favourite food that he often wants to ask for, Peter says 'nana' for all foods and drinks, except milk for which he makes a particular sign with his hand. He also uses a sign that his mother recognises as meaning 'more'. All vehicles are symbolised by a sound similar to a car's engine and the sight of any real or toy vehicle with wheels will prompt Peter to make the sound. He will continue to make it as he rides in a car or bus or plays with toy tractors, diggers or trains.

As the first words Peter recognised as describing an action he desired from his mother were 'Would you like to come up?', he uses the word 'Up' to mean 'Please pick me up', raising his arms and holding them out to a familiar adult. He does the same thing when he means 'Please cuddle me', 'Please let me sit on your lap', 'Please carry me' or 'Please comfort me'.

Thus, with a vocabulary of just six words and sounds and a few actions and expressions, Peter is already able to communicate successfully with his parents, brother and other familiar caregivers, because they are aware of his needs as an individual and willing to anticipate and make educated guesses.

If this continues, with adults and older children offering more words to describe what Peter wants to communicate to them and rewarding his efforts to speak by giving him what he asks for or joining in with his play, he will be motivated to learn more words and continue to make the effort to speak. His confidence and control will develop with practice and he will gradually use more and more verbal communication and probably feel less need to rely on signs, although symbolic sounds will continue to play a large part in his role play and small world play.

Twelve months to eighteen months

Different languages contain different numbers of sounds. English uses more than 40 sounds, but many languages have fewer. Some sounds are common to most languages, while others occur in only a few.

Babies and young children are able to reproduce all of the sounds required to speak in any language, so no language is too difficult for them to learn and absorb. Speaking two or more languages fluently is a great asset in today's world and the best time to learn them is while you are very young and eager to embrace all new experiences. Bilingual families should always share their first language, as well as the language of the country they are living in, with their children from the beginning, teaching both languages equally while the children are learning to speak and understand. It is much harder to learn an additional language at a later stage of life.

In all languages, beginning with vowel sounds and combining them with the simplest consonants, such as 'd', 'm' and 'b', leads young children to first attempt words such as 'mama', 'dada' and 'baba'. When parents choose to recognise these words as referring to themselves and their children, they react with pleasure and this provides the reward that encourages the children to continue to attempt to speak and communicate.

Phrases and sentences

Between twelve and eighteen months, toddlers gradually become more skilled at naming the people, animals and objects they point to and at requesting more information from those around them, which they absorb rapidly and easily. During this period they also learn to understand simple instructions, such as: 'Find your shoes' or 'Give this to Granny', and to carry them out. A favourite request for most children seems to be 'Put this in the bin' and they may enjoy taking pieces of scrap paper to a wastepaper basket, one at a time, for several minutes.

Single words, such as Mummy, Daddy, baby, cat, dog, car, tractor, shoe and drink, can now be combined and expanded to form two- and three-word phrases. Adults should respond to a child's single words by repeating them and adding to them, in order to correct pronunciation, put the words into context, make connections and develop thinking skills.

If a child says 'Baby', an adult can reply, 'Baby's asleep. Shush, let's be quiet'.

An offer of 'Cat' can be expanded to, 'The cat has soft fur. We can stroke her gently'.

Recognising and saying 'Tractor' can lead to, 'We saw a tractor in the field yesterday and here's a tractor on the road today'.

There is no need for adults to simplify their own speech any further, but it is important to appreciate children's attempts at speech and to offer relevant comments and information that will interest them. Repetition, a calm and measured pace and an encouraging tone of voice are the most important tools for teaching and supporting speech development, but enthusiasm is also important. If children are ignored when they begin to speak, not understood or corrected harshly, they will give up and stop trying.

Children who use single words and receive attentive and relevant responses from primary caregivers will quickly move on to forming phrases, such as 'Baby sleep', 'Cat, soft fur' and 'Tractor road'. They will begin to copy and use phrases that they hear often, such as 'All gone', 'Oh dear' and 'No more'. They will instinctively pick out the nouns and the more important adjectives and verbs to say first, but they will be absorbing the connectives and the form and pattern of their language, so that they will be ready to use it later.

Children may learn two or more languages alongside each other and select words and phrases from each to use and practise at different times or with different people. Listening to favourite songs on CDs can also help children to learn about words, rhythm and fluency, but they are not a substitute for human interaction and singing or chanting with caregivers.

Finger rhymes and action songs are extremely valuable when introduced to and shared with children from eighteen months or younger. They can help children to learn and remember the meanings of words, practise co-ordinated movements and begin to anticipate what comes next, take cues and join in.

Understanding medical conditions

Many children suffer from minor medical conditions, which can cause them discomfort and prevent them from taking advantage of all opportunities. It is important for parents and carers to be aware of their needs and minimise the disruptions as far as possible. If children have eczema they will need to be distracted from scratching their skin and offered a variety of strategies to avoid or overcome discomfort, as well as any cream that has been prescribed. Those with hay fever may need to learn when it is best to stay indoors and any activities to avoid, as well as how to use tissues effectively. Children affected

Twelve months to eighteen months

by cerebral palsy will not cope well if they become too cold and may need adaptations to their homes and early years settings.

Children should be helped to learn when and how to ask for their particular medications or any assistance that they need from as early an age as possible, but adults must recognise and meet their needs before they are able to do this.

> Eilidh, aged sixteen months, suffers from asthma but, as her speech and language skills are not yet well developed, she is not able to tell her carers when she begins to feel uncomfortable at the beginning of an attack. However, her key person at nursery watches her carefully and is aware of her body language.
>
> When breathing becomes more difficult for Eilidh, she starts to be irritable and gives up on her play activity. If she is outside she usually goes indoors. She rubs at her chin, neck or chest and sits or lies down. She may begin to cough, but will refuse a drink if it is offered as she is unable to swallow liquids at this time.
>
> If her discomfort progresses further, she will begin to suck her hand and breathe with her mouth open, gasping for air, before an audible wheeze is heard. But her carer ensures that she fetches Eilidh's inhaler and gives her the medication early enough, so that the attack rarely reaches this stage.

It is important always to be aware of the body language of young children as they will express their feelings of pleasure or discomfort very obviously, even before they are able to talk. This is particularly important when living or working with children with specific medical needs, as the adapting of the environment or activities and the administering of the correct medication at the appropriate times will make all the difference to managing the conditions and minimizing the disruption to the children's lives.

If carers always provide medication when it is needed, in a calm and matter-of-fact manner, explaining how they know that it is needed, why it is important and how much better it will make the children feel, the child will naturally begin to recognise and understand their own symptoms as they grow older and ask for their medication when they need it. Setting this example within a home or early years setting will also encourage other children to learn how to read body language, to recognise and empathise with the needs of others and to offer help or support when appropriate. This will ensure that all children recognise that people have different needs and strive to achieve full inclusion within any group.

Songs, rhymes and playtimes

By the age of eighteen months, many children will recognise familiar songs and rhymes and have some favourites that they may ask for with words or actions. They will join in and chant or sing along with older children, adults or CDs. They will also join in with familiar stories and fill in missing words or sounds when the reader pauses at significant points. Songs, rhymes and stories are an important and enjoyable way of learning and practising vocabulary, enunciation and fluency and may be particularly helpful to those who are learning two or more languages.

During their second year of life children can learn a great deal from playing with others, particularly older siblings and friends. The babies and toddlers can be introduced to sharing toys, giving, taking and swapping, offering playthings to others and communicating through smiles, gestures, sounds and

Figure 3.5 Siblings need opportunities to play together in order to form strong and healthy relationships.

words. These relaxed playtimes can offer children the warm and rewarding feelings that promote an understanding of why and how they should seek social interactions and will drive them to initiate and respond to the advances of their families, carers, friends and peers. Strong bonds can be formed at this stage that will ensure healthy sibling relationships and invaluable friendships during the years that follow.

> Taeko, aged seventeen months, wants to join in with her brother, Seiji, aged three years and two months, who is making a picture with stickers. He is willing to let her share, placing the box of stickers fairly between them on the floor and passing her a sheet of paper. Taeko tries to peel off the backing and apply the stickers but finds this too difficult and picks up the box to shake it instead. Seiji takes it back and puts it down in its place, saying 'I need it there. You can share too, but you have to keep the box here'. He repeats this firmly when Taeko picks up the box again and, this time, she becomes angry and throws a handful of stickers onto the floor.
>
> Luckily, her father is watching and listening and understands both children's frustrations, so he steps in to help them. First, he praises Seiji for explaining sensibly to Taeko and not being cross with her, admires the picture he is making and replaces the box in the correct place. Then, he helps Taeko to peel the backing from some stickers and shows her how to make a picture too, telling her that she should ask Seiji to help her if she can't do what he is doing.

Frustrations, control and safety

At around this age children can become frustrated by their inability to make themselves fully understood and to communicate all of their thoughts, needs and wishes. This may cause tears, tantrums and uncooperative behaviour, making it the beginning of a challenging period for parents and carers, but these are necessary because the strong feelings are what will drive the children to want to learn to communicate more fully. It can be observed that some children with special or additional needs do not suffer the same angry, frustrated or impatient feelings and so appear happier and less challenging, but they do not learn and develop at the depth or pace of their peers, partially because they lack the strong desire and determination to do so.

Active communication involves watching and listening in order to understand the situation from the child's point of view and respecting their feelings when they express themselves verbally or non-verbally. Adults must put aside their own feelings, views and opinions and allow children to say or show how they feel without interruption before responding sensitively and appropriately.

After the age of twelve months, and certainly by eighteen months, children need to understand and respond to the word 'No' for their own safety. Most children will usually do this, although they cannot be completely reliable at this age and, at times, will be too fascinated or distracted to comply quickly. Other useful words and phrases that parents and carers may wish to teach their children to respond to are: 'Stop', 'Give it to me', 'Leave it alone', 'Hold my hand', 'I'm coming', 'Wait a minute'.

Some adults may feel overwhelmed by the task of controlling and safeguarding children from this age, while still keeping them happy and stimulated. It is important to remember that, although small children's presences can be huge to those who care for them, they are still little and in need of love and protection. A good way to be reminded of who are the adults is to watch the children sleeping or to pick them up and carry them and give them a cuddle.

It can be difficult to strike the right balance between keeping very young children safe and allowing them to explore and discover, because they have endless curiosity but little coordination and no experience. Adults must help them to predict outcomes, prevent accidents and avoid disasters, but encourage investigations and gradually increasing independence, thus offering protection and support without stifling creativity and confidence.

Branching out
Eighteen months to twenty-four months

Some young children love to please adults and do not worry about making mistakes as they learn to speak. These children add a new word or two to their vocabularies every day and gradually begin to put them together and create phrases for their own use, copying all of the words and sounds that they hear. Others seem determined to practise words and phrases on their own and only speak out once they are sure that the words they want to say are correct. These are the two basic ways in which children learn to speak and most children fall into one category or the other, although there are a few exceptions and some experience phases of one attitude and then the other.

Reluctant speech

Parents or carers who worry that their children are not yet speaking very much might try standing and listening quietly just outside the door of a room in which their children are playing. They may discover that the children are busy practising some new, more complicated sentences or phrases, which they will use as soon as they feel confident. The rewards of praise and attention from a primary caregiver are all the incentive a small child needs to feel encouraged to continue working on verbal communication skills. Using opening statements that invite the child to talk, such as: 'I'm trying to remember which books we read yesterday' or 'I wonder what we could build with the bricks' can be a very useful technique.

Some toddlers who are unwilling to speak to adults or older children may find their voices when they spend time in the company of babies. Knowing that they have superior skills, and that the younger children cannot judge

Eighteen months to twenty-four months

Figure 4.1 Toddlers may develop their self-confidence and communication skills through speaking to babies.

them but will be happy to be spoken to, may give them the self-confidence they need to overcome their natural reticence and respond to the babies' desire for communication. The smiles, sounds and gestures that the babies offer provide instant gratification and encourage the communication to continue as it is rewarding for all participants.

> Jacob, aged nineteen months, enjoys exploring and naming toys. He has absorbed the names of favourite objects, which have been given to him by his family, and is confident that he will be understood and praised when he speaks. He picks up toys and shows them to others, saying 'Tractor' or 'Car', or places the receiver of a toy telephone to his ear and says 'Hiya'.
>
> He asks for new words and names by making connections and guesses and waiting for an adult to supply the word he needs. For example, he holds up a toy aeroplane, touches the propeller and says 'Copter?' His mother shows him that a helicopter's propeller is on top, but this one is at the front and tells him that this is a plane. She also shows him how to fly the plane and make swooping sounds. Jacob is delighted with this new concept and holds the plane first one way and

Eighteen months to twenty-four months

then the other, repeating the words and making sounds as he makes the plane fly through the air.

When he is helped to build a track for his trains, Jacob puts the engines onto the track and pushes them along, making 'choo choo' sounds. After a short while, he says 'Grandad!' He has independently remembered that his Grandad has a collection of trains and a track layout at his house and that he enjoys playing trains with Grandad. This connection is reinforced when his Grandma says 'Yes, Grandad would like to see your train track wouldn't he?' Jacob nods and puts together his words and sounds 'Grandad – choo choo!'

Later, Jacob sees a box of biscuits in his mother's bag and takes them out, saying 'Mmmm'. But, when his mother takes the box and says 'All gone! Never mind, we'll have lunch soon', Jacob accepts this statement as true and turns back to his play. As his parents use simple phrases like this consistently, he is able to understand and feel secure.

Gradually, two- and three-word phrases will develop further to include connectives and conjunctions, until children are speaking in simple sentences most of the time. Some of these will be sentences that they have learned and copied from parents and carers, such as: 'It's bath time now' or 'The car's in the garage'. Others may come from favourite stories, rhymes or songs and will be spoken with the appropriate inflections, chanted rhythmically or sung, displaying some knowledge of the beat or tune.

Children will often use the words they have to describe situations as they see them, before they become aware of variations within their language. A toddler may see somebody laughing and declare loudly, 'He's a funny man!' To avoid any offence being taken, the child's parent or carer will need to supply the correct variation quickly and in a positive tone, 'Yes, the man is laughing because it's funny'.

Throughout this period, children will continue to stumble over some words and retain some infantilisms. Families may enjoy these and even adopt one or two of them to be used at home for years. The mixing up of sounds or words occasionally does not harm speech development and should only be corrected, in a calm and matter-of-fact manner, if it bothers the child. Putting pressure upon children to speak too correctly, or laughing at them, makes them feel tense and afraid to make mistakes while they are young and can lead to a lack of self-confidence, a reluctance or refusal to speak or a temporary stammer.

Having previously mastered the ability to produce vowel sounds and the simplest consonants, children of this age will rapidly add the other sounds they need to speak in their first language. In English these will usually be 'p', 't' and 'w', followed by the other phonetic sounds represented by single letters.

> Oliver, aged twenty-two months, is visiting a friend with his Grandma and follows her into the kitchen when she goes to make some drinks and snacks. He is impatient to begin as soon as he sees the food being prepared, but is happily distracted by her enthusiastic running commentary on each item and the bowls and plates needed.
>
> He watches her take a spoon from the drawer to stir the coffee and asks for a spoon too. He is allowed to choose one and now asks to stir the drinks. She explains that the coffee is too hot to touch, but suggests that he might like to stir something else and offers some choices. Oliver chooses to stir the strawberries and solemnly does so for nearly a minute, being very careful to stir gently and to keep them in the bowl. He is very happy when he is praised for his stirring and asked to carry the bowl of strawberries to the table and show them to his Grandma.

Rising twos can spend a lot of time feeling frustrated and exhibiting challenging behaviour. Helping them to communicate their wishes clearly and easily, both verbally and in other ways, will make the most difficult phase as short as possible and allow more time for enjoying activities together. If adults offer small responses to show that they are listening and interested when children speak, they are more likely to continue to make the effort to communicate effectively. Maintaining eye contact and using small nods and vocal sounds can both soothe and encourage children when they are struggling to develop conversational skills.

Eighteen months to twenty-four months

Figure 4.2 Adults should help children to communicate their wishes and make time to enjoy activities together.

Offering choices

As children become more able to express their views, they wish to make more choices for themselves and are also more likely to defy authority or refuse demands. This can be exhausting for their carers at times, but the way to retain a close and constructive relationship is to keep communicating and to offer firm and fair discipline in a calm and loving manner. Being able to talk and to understand each other will ensure that children's valuable growing independence is supported along with their communication, social and emotional skills.

If young children are offered only verbal choices they will often just repeat the items at random or choose the last one because they cannot remember the others. At this age they cannot retain a list of similar items in their heads and make a choice between them. Offering visual clues, such as objects or pictures, allows children to look from one to another to reconsider each option several times and then to make an informed choice. They may also

Eighteen months to twenty-four months

choose in practical ways, by fetching a toy or garment from the cupboard or selecting a book from the shelf.

Not talking very much at this age need not always be a cause for concern, but not understanding what is said is a far more serious indicator of delayed development. The sustained repeating of words and sounds, as in echolalia, can be a sign of a disability or disorder.

Routine is of paramount importance for children nearing two years of age. They need the security of expecting what might happen soon and knowing what will happen later. They also need support in learning to plan actions and activities for themselves. Adults can help by putting familiar sequences into words that the children understand and repeating them frequently, so that instructions are absorbed and memories retained. Once they have enough of these, children are able to begin to make predictions and plans of their own.

Children of this age continue to collect names and labels for everything and everybody they know and their memory capacity for these can seem almost

Figure 4.3 Young children can learn to recognise and name colours through using coloured pencils and crayons.

infinite. They also begin to create questions and different types of comments by using appropriate intonations and inflections within their speech. Although many mistakes are still made, in pronunciation, grammar and word order, they often try to self-correct and repeat statements or questions several times until they are satisfied that they sound right.

Adults and older children may play enjoyable games with toddlers to help them to learn names and labels. They can point to pictures or photographs for them to name and then ask them to find pictures or photographs and point to them in turn, or use real objects, people or animals. They may move on to finding colours or matching items. Using coloured pencils or crayons is an enjoyable way for toddlers to explore colours and learn their names.

Questions to extend learning

Before the age of two years children can learn and remember the words for objects that are not visible to them and for concepts as well as concrete objects. Holding a mental image in mind, to picture and describe what they want, they will be able to ask for a toy that is out of sight in a cupboard or toy box, a blanket that has been left in their bedroom or a favourite book that was put away on a shelf. They will ask to use the swing in the garden, to visit Granny or to see the squirrels at the park. Adults can build on this activity and extend vocabulary and thinking skills by asking appropriate questions and modelling relevant responses. For example, an adult might ask: 'We put your train in this toy box when we tidied up yesterday, didn't we? Shall we open the lid and find it?' or 'Did we leave the blanket on your bed? I think teddy's looking after it there, isn't he?'

Being aware of all potential possibilities can allow parents and carers to extend learning further. If children are keen to go out, time, other commitments or the weather may be important considerations. An adult may ask: 'Shall we look outside? Can you see through the window? It's been raining! Everything's wet and there are puddles. What do we need to wear if we go out? Can you remember where your boots are?'

Encouraging children to stop and think and to link thoughts and memories allows them to begin to understand and use skills in logic and reasoning. Some may even begin to develop early signs of common sense!

Very young children prefer to hear and respond well to child-directed speech, with words spoken more clearly, at a higher pitch and with careful or even exaggerated pronunciation, lively inflections and enough repetition. However, they benefit enormously from hearing adults and older children using full sentences with correct grammar, rather than just separate words or only simple short phrases.

Hearing impairment

There are many degrees of hearing impairment and some children may suffer from mild or moderate hearing loss, while others have more severe hearing loss or are totally deaf. Many others suffer temporary or variable hearing loss during their early years, due to glue ear and similar conditions, when they have a cold or other minor illness. Being unable to hear clearly makes learning to speak and understand much more difficult. Those who cannot hear speech or sounds at all may be unable to learn to speak or to participate in many activities enjoyed by their peers during this period.

Those with mild to moderate hearing loss may be helped by sympathetic understanding and measures such as the removal of unnecessary background noise and slow, clear speech that is carefully enunciated. Adults should invite children to go with them to a quieter area, come down to their level and face them while speaking, repeating words and sentences as often as necessary. They should attract their attention before beginning to speak, perhaps by using their names or the word 'listen', and be aware that group instructions will probably be missed by these children, so they should be informed individually of what is going to happen or what they need to do.

When there is more severe hearing loss, or an inability to hear any useful sounds, the adults caring for the children must find other ways to communicate to prevent the children from becoming frustrated or isolated. They may learn a sign language with the children and also use mimes, actions and expressions to emphasise their meanings. They may eventually learn to speak, but this will require intensive work with speech therapists and will happen later in life.

Eighteen months to twenty-four months

> Ben, aged twenty-three months, is profoundly deaf. He uses mimes and actions to communicate his needs and wishes and is beginning to understand and use some Makaton signs. His parents request a place for him at a day nursery and staff decide to place him with the two to three year olds, as this will be safer for him than with the younger children and will avoid the need for him to go through a transition during the next year.
>
> The day nursery staff use Makaton signs, which are performed alongside the spoken words, when they communicate with Ben on his own and when they speak with a group that includes him. The other children accept that Ben does not speak to them and begin to copy staff and use mimes and signs when including him in their play. Ben bends his knees and bounces when he wants to play on the trampoline in the garden and Harry, aged two years and two months, takes his hand and leads him over to it. Georgia, aged three years, offers Ben a drum and a beater and shows him how to use them. Ben bangs the drum enthusiastically and smiles at Georgia. She smiles back at him and claps her hands, then tries to beat her drum in time with his.

Although it will be important for the adults in an early years setting to know of any special or additional needs in order to promote full inclusion, there will be no need for practitioners to engage in lengthy explanations with young children. One and two year olds have no preconceptions of people's abilities and do not assume that everybody is the same. They will learn about each other as individuals and often find their own ways to communicate, as well as following the examples of the adults around them. Using signs, speech, mimes, actions and the language of smiles, laughter and hugs will ensure a rich and inclusive environment.

Children can learn about each other and take their first steps towards forming friendships independently if they regularly spend time playing in pairs and small groups, supported by interested and sympathetic adults. They should be encouraged to take turns to speak and to learn to listen to and think about what others say and respond to them appropriately, rather than making comments at random or talking over each other.

By the age of two years, most children should understand that communication is a two-way process and will be willing to try to accept that others may have different points of view to share. The early skills of turn taking and developing an understanding of what other people are saying, and what they are possibly thinking, will be vitally important in forming and maintaining relationships throughout life.

Siblings, friendships and social skills

Toddlers may communicate their desire to join in with the play of older siblings at home or with older friends in an early years setting by copying what they do, whether they fully understand the game or not. Young children may watch others putting on oven gloves before handling toy food and baking trays when playing in a role-play kitchen. On another occasion, the toddlers may put on an oven glove when entering the kitchen area, but then proceed to pick up all of the toy food with the other hand, proving that they do not yet understand the significance of wearing an oven glove, but that they are aware of others, are carefully observing their play and are keen to learn and be a part of the group. These are the more important skills to develop; the details will follow naturally in due course.

Figure 4.4 Families should seek older role models who are prepared to guide their young children in playing cooperatively.

Eighteen months to twenty-four months

The safety of very young children is paramount and the toys and equipment offered to them must be age appropriate, particularly if they may play unsupervised for short periods. However, they can enjoy toys and activities intended for older children and learn a great deal from them at times when they play together with older siblings, cousins or friends who are able to supervise and safeguard the little ones responsibly.

Through sharing games with older children, toddlers can develop physical, intellectual, emotional and social skills that they will then go on to use when interacting with their peers. They will learn how to express their wishes and feelings in acceptable ways and understand how to communicate with people of various ages.

Parents and carers should aim to provide older role models for their young children, who are prepared to play cooperatively and guide gently, setting a good example to be imitated and followed and showing the little ones how to have more fun and avoid upsets by communicating effectively and considering others. As far as possible, they should steer their children away from older ones who may set an undesirable example of behaviour, control or consideration, or encourage over-excitement, poor communication skills or a lack of good manners.

> Ellen, aged two years, has invented her own game to play with her baby sister, Daisy, aged nine months. She attracts the baby's attention when they are sitting together at the table or in the car and says, 'Let's play laughing!'
>
> She hides her face and then pops up to surprise Daisy and laughs. The baby copies Ellen by looking away and back again and laughing. The game can continue for several minutes.

Siblings can build and share special relationships from a very young age, provided that they frequently spend periods of time together in familiar situations. Adults should avoid always rushing in with toys or distractions and should not feel that they must be interacting with small children all the time. Sometimes it is fine to stand back at a short distance and appear not to be paying close attention.

Eighteen months to twenty-four months

Figure 4.5 Children who play together regularly can build special relationships and create their own games.

It is important to allow siblings and friends to spend time together regularly, when they are safely supervised but have to create their own entertainment. Sharing the small moments between the routines of each day will ensure that healthy and rewarding relationships are developed and nurtured, from the early days of laughing with a baby to the avid conversations of later years.

Fighting for independence
Two years to two and a half years

It is vital to share books and stories with children from a very early age. Hearing and enjoying words and language in this way enables babies and children to name and label objects, learn and practise vocabulary, put words together, absorb grammar and sentence structure, use logic and reason, develop imagination and enjoy the richness of flowing language.

Introducing too many new words at once can be confusing and too difficult for young children to separate, define and remember. Offering one or two new names or concepts at a time, among the familiar ones, will enable children to absorb them easily and learn to use them confidently. Small children love to hear the same story or song over and over again. They feel close to their families and regular carers through frequently sharing familiar jokes and phrases, and find comfort and security by following the same routines each day and maintaining consistent expectations.

Repetition is important to enable children to learn both words and sentence structure. Listening to the same story many times gradually teaches children how to predict language patterns and join in. Pausing before key words and allowing children to supply them, or making eye contact with the children and chanting favourite phrases together, is not only enjoyable but also helps them to gradually absorb new ideas and embed a strong understanding of how language works. Using appropriate stories and poems can also teach the concepts of rhyme and alliteration.

> Reading a new storybook, Chloe, aged two years, is fascinated by a joyful picture of a 'giraffe in the bath who likes to laugh'. She studies the picture carefully and listens as the words are read to her several

Two years to two and a half years

times. Then she places her finger on the page, traces the bubbles rising up from the bath tub and says 'Tickles'. By herself, she has made the connection that the giraffe might be laughing because he is being tickled by the bubbles in the bath.

She is delighted when an adult puts her idea into a sentence for her, saying 'Yes, the giraffe is laughing because the bubbles are tickling him'. She is now able to say, 'Tickle bubbles giraffe' and she will go on thinking about and refining her phrase each time she looks at the book.

Challenging behaviour and boundaries

Frustrations still occur regularly during these months but, if children's communication skills are well developed, they are more able to put their problems into words and explain what they want. They will push boundaries, both to satisfy their developing independence and to check that there are still firm rules that make them feel safe and secure. They will often, but not always, accept 'No' from an adult caregiver and will sometimes tell themselves 'No' and be able to regulate their own behaviour, stopping themselves from doing something that they would like to do but must not, such as touching the glass cupboard door or emptying their drinks out onto the table.

Olivia, aged two years and two months, has learned to say 'No' and to use other words to reinforce her wishes. She is able to understand simple instructions and choices, but also to decide whether she will comply or resist. She enjoys walking up and downstairs at home and would like to do it repeatedly.

When her mother does not have time to supervise this, she tells Olivia that she must decide to go up or down and stay there for a while because it is not safe to play on the stairs. Sometimes Olivia will agree, choose 'Up' or 'Down' and walk sensibly. At other times she will say 'Coming down', then 'Going up' and change her mind frequently, until she is removed from the stairs and distracted with a different activity. Her mood and reaction cannot be predicted in advance.

Two years to two and a half years

For some parents and carers the newly developing independence of their two year olds, which causes more challenging behaviour, can come as a surprise or even a shock. They may also find that their children continue to behave well when they are out or in the company of other people, but often lose control or exhibit defiance at home.

People may offer compliments or suggest that they are 'lucky' because their children are well-behaved and often refuse to believe that they are actually demanding and difficult to manage at home. Of course, having two year olds who control their behaviour and observe acceptable social standards is never down to luck and these adults should actually be congratulated on having put in the hard work and consistently provided the good examples and correct guidance. They should also be offered understanding and support in managing the times when their delightful and amenable children temporarily become completely unreasonable or inconsolable.

If asked to consider whether they would rather that their children behaved well outside the home or in private, parents and carers will understand and agree that it is better for children to make extra efforts towards 'best behaviour' when in certain public situations, but then become themselves again as soon as they are able to because they feel that their primary carers provide a safe haven in which they can let go. They may have a need to release some pressure through more challenging behaviour when alone with their family at home.

When they take out their frustrations on their mother, father, grandparent, nanny or childminder, they are demonstrating that they feel secure in this person's care and sure that they will experience unconditional love, no matter how they behave. Understanding this can enable the adults to take the tantrums as a compliment rather than as a personal attack! They can then continue to reassure the children of their loving care, set appropriate boundaries and model desirable behaviour.

Digital media and popular characters

Two year olds may begin to take an interest in the television programmes and DVDs created for young children, especially if they have older siblings. Watching these regularly with the children for short periods can provide valuable stimuli for discussion and opportunities to practise memory skills. Children may also begin to recognise similarities and differences between real

Two years to two and a half years

objects, animals and people, pictures in books and photographs, toys and characters seen on screens.

If parents and carers prefer not to use television or DVDs with their young children, they might consider allowing them to listen to stories on CDs as this is an opportunity for them to hear normal speech flowing around them but not directed exclusively at them. This can aid children's understanding of fluency, inflection and intonation and give them an appropriate idea of what they will aim to achieve as they grow older. This can be particularly valuable for first and only children who do not hear the normal conversations that flow over those in larger, busy families, and should definitely be considered for those with mild forms of speech delay.

However, families and practitioners should avoid leaving a television or radio on in the background or playing music and story CDs continuously. Adults and children should watch or listen together and then turn off the programme or selection. It is important that adults set an appropriate example, so that children can learn how to choose what to watch or listen to and when to do so. Meals and activities can sometimes be planned in advance

Figure 5.1 Dressing up as different characters can encourage children to try out different sounds and voices.

51

to fit around favourite programmes, or a special time planned within a daily schedule for sharing a DVD. Providing character dressing-up outfits can also encourage young children to try out different sounds and voices and to re-create favourite stories or songs or make up their own.

Listening to songs, music or stories may be an enjoyable accompaniment to construction play, making jigsaw puzzles or craft activities at times, but they should not always be used as they can distract children from becoming truly absorbed in their own thoughts or prevent spontaneous conversations and descriptions.

When living or working with children who are developing their speech skills, adults must reduce background noise and ensure some periods of quiet, especially when speaking to children, talking together while playing, teaching new songs or rhymes, reading stories or listening to sounds outside.

> When Isla, aged two years and four months, receives a box of farm animals as a present, she points to the horse and the goat and gives them the names of these animals in her favourite television programme. She then names the programme. When she is asked whether a dog and a pig are in the programme too, she is able to name those characters and look for the animals in the box.

Favourite characters can first become recognisable and important to children around the time of their second birthday. Merchandise such as books, toys, television programmes, DVDs, games, puzzles, CDs, bags, lunchboxes and clothing will begin to compete for their attention and they will start to take notice of what is available and draw parents' and carers' attention to the items that they find attractive. The concept of making choices outside homes or early years settings may now be carefully introduced and children guided towards choosing sensibly and looking for what they need rather than allowing themselves to be persuaded to want large quantities of consumer items.

In the same way as offering a selection of snacks in the nursery or a choice of t-shirts at home, adults may take children to a shop to buy a new lunchbox or a more difficult jigsaw puzzle and allow them to choose one featuring their favourite character. They can be encouraged to plan a shopping trip in advance, told that they will find the item they need to bring home today and,

Two years to two and a half years

if they see toys, books, DVDs or other things that they like very much, they can ask for them to be written down and remembered as possible birthday or Christmas presents.

Although the adults may then need to return to the shops fairly quickly to buy the proposed gifts before they become unavailable, they can do so without the children and hide them away to be kept as a surprise, thus allowing the children to understand and practise waiting for items that are desirable but not essential. This communicates to the children that shopping can be fun and there are many desirable purchases that can be made, but that there is a difference between needing something and merely wanting it and we cannot always have everything that we want. Committed parents and carers must strive to give their children everything they need and some of the things they would like to have.

Children over two are able to remember events from the recent past and to follow regular routines, with some reminders and support. They will also make statements that prove they are making their own connections between people, toys, events, books, songs and favourite television programmes or DVDs. Favourite songs, rhymes and stories are likely to be firmly established, although new ones are also eagerly received, and the children are likely to be

Figure 5.2 Favourite characters can gradually become recognisable and important to two year olds.

Two years to two and a half years

happy to recite and sing alone, sometimes to other people. They may enjoy drawing and modelling but are no longer satisfied with just coloured marks and scribbles or undefined shapes in clay or playdough, so they will suggest their own ideas for pictures and models and ask for help to create them.

Imaginative role play

Two year olds often talk to themselves while playing, especially during construction and small world play. They may describe what they are doing, ask questions or say what they are trying to achieve: 'I'm making a tall tower', 'Where's the red door?', 'I want this track to go to the station'. They may speak for their characters: 'I'm going to bed now' or 'I want to go outside', or about them: 'They're all going for a walk' or 'The builders are digging the road'.

Play people, animals and vehicles are popular with children of all ages but small parts must be removed when offered to under-threes and adult supervision provided continuously.

Whenever possible, parents and carers should spend periods of uninterrupted close time with children, chatting, singing and talking about relevant things while playing. At this young age the children need to watch people's

Figure 5.3 Small world play provides opportunities for children to explore and direct imaginary worlds.

Two years to two and a half years

mouth movements while they talk and concentrate on developing their speech within a relaxed atmosphere.

Role play can take off at this stage and the children may move quickly from copying an adult feeding teddies and dollies with plastic spoons to creating

Figure 5.4 Providing pretend food for toys is a popular early role-play game.

a busy picnic or tea party and preparing a selection of pretend food on a toy cooker. Talking is important to these games, so they provide a rewarding way of practising communication skills, especially if two or more children play together.

Adults or older children can provide new ideas and demonstrate how to talk for and with soft toys, small world characters, puppets, babies or pets, providing humour, imagination and greater understanding. They can also help with negotiations when necessary to enable cooperative group play. Young children adore games in which adults talk for a number of characters in different voices, making the stories repetitive and funny. Some minor disagreements presented jokingly are hilarious to children at this age and help them to practise verbalising feelings and emotions.

For example, an adult may play with a small-world farm set and create a joking conversation, with actions, between a farmer and a pig:

'Now you go back to your field.'
'I don't want to go to the field. I want to roll in the mud.'
'You can't roll in the mud; it's time for your lunch.'
'Yes I can! Look! I rolled in the mud.'
'Now you're all muddy and you won't be able to eat your lunch nicely. Go back to your field!'
'I don't want to. I'll jump into the river to wash the mud off. Now I've had a swim and I'm clean!'
'Yes, you are clean. Now go back to your field please.'
'All right, I will go back to my field now.'
'Thank you. I think it's time you had a little sleep!'

Two year olds will watch and listen to a simple game like this for two or three minutes and become completely absorbed in the characters and ideas being created. When it ends they are quite likely to say, 'Tell me that again!' or 'Play the farmer game again!'

Whether the adults repeat the games, vary them or create new ideas, the children will enjoy them all and eventually reproduce such games for themselves. Importantly, they will go on to create their own imaginative games as they grow older, using the ideas that first inspired them, and retain the ability to enjoy details and laugh at situations. In a competitive and often unfair world, a strong and creative imagination and a sense of humour are vital for happiness and success.

Fluent speech and social conventions

Between two and two and a half years many children make the transition from naming things and copying phrases to fluent speech, although, for some, this stage comes a little later. They are now able to ask and answer questions, make choices and express opinions. Their sentences are clearer and more carefully planned and their vocabularies and understanding are increasing rapidly. However, they need enough time to think and it is important to allow them time to process information and work out what is being asked of them, before insisting that they hurry to begin or complete a task that they do not yet fully understand.

Using open-ended questions, rather than the kind that invite only yes or no answers, can encourage further speech development, but it is important not to bombard children with questions and to accept that some periods of silence may be necessary and constructive within conversations. If children feel overwhelmed by the amount of information requested of them, have to try to rush to answer each question before another is asked or become confused, the ideas that they wanted to communicate may be lost. This may discourage them from trying to talk openly with an adult in the future.

Children of this age should be intelligible to familiar adults and older siblings, although strangers may not understand much of what they say. They will continue to use some infantilisms and specific sounds, words, phrases or expressions that they expect their families and carers to interpret correctly. When trying out new vocabulary they may shorten longer words to their last sounds, as these are the parts that they hear most clearly and that their memories are able to retain.

In order to develop clear and accurate speech with confidence and without frustration, children must have good hearing that allows them to hear clearly, reliably and at an appropriate and consistent volume. Intermittent hearing loss, due to colds, infections and a condition known as 'glue ear', causes problems for many children who do not have a permanent hearing impairment.

Parents and carers should investigate further if children use muffled, unclear, confused or inaccurate speech, if they always speak very loudly and enjoy loud sounds or do not react with surprise to sudden very loud noises, if they turn up the volume of a television, radio or CD player or sit very close to the machine or speaker, if they do not respond when called or spoken to, if they often misunderstand instructions or if they frequently say 'Pardon?' or 'What?'

Two years to two and a half years

A GP will be able to advise whether any medications or further investigations could help a child struggling with a 'glue ear' condition or variable hearing loss during the most vital period for the development of speech and language, understanding and communication.

> Callum, aged two years and three months, is encouraged to share toys, treats and adult attention with his baby brother, Rory, aged eleven months. He gives Rory some bricks to play with while he is building a model, then offers him some plastic spoons to help to stir the pretend soup he is making and lifts the bowl down from the play cooker, putting it on the floor so that Rory can reach it.
>
> Then Callum decides to draw a picture and sits at his small table. When Rory pulls himself up to stand at the table beside him, Callum pushes some paper towards him and hands him a pencil. At this point, his nanny has to intervene before Rory puts the pencil into his mouth or pokes it into his eye. She takes the pencil, saying, 'That is kind of you, Callum, but Rory still needs help with pencils'. She helps Rory to make a few marks and then removes the pencil and offers another toy to encourage him to play on the floor again.
>
> After this, Callum fetches the collection of conkers that he picked up in the park. As he is about to hold one out to Rory, his nanny has to say, 'No, don't share that with the baby'.

It is important to encourage sharing and playing together from a very young age, but many explanations will also be needed as the mixed messages that it is good to share but that some things cannot be shared are very confusing for a two year old. Adults need to talk about how babies put everything into their mouths and how they cannot be as careful as bigger boys and girls. They should help children to think of the things that might be dangerous for babies, such as conkers and other garden items, pencils and pens, small pieces, bendy things and sharp things, and to try to remember to consider this before offering items to share. However, they cannot yet be trusted to make appropriate decisions or remember rules, so close adult supervision is always required when toddlers are playing freely on the floor near to babies.

Two years to two and a half years

Figure 5.5 Toddlers enjoy communicating through parallel play and quiet thinking time alongside their carers.

Toddlers enjoy parallel play with adults, siblings or peers. They welcome periods of silence for thinking and will speak when they want to, so carers should not talk too much of the time or constantly ask questions. This can actually prevent absorption in play and the possibility of spontaneous verbal communication, and weaken a developing bond with a child. Sharing toys and demonstrating shared interests are very valuable forms of communication, although they are non-verbal.

Parents and carers may now encourage children to use the words 'please' and 'thank you' appropriately and support them in learning other social conventions that occur within their culture, such as, for example, 'excuse me'. Children may also be prepared to repeat some phrases upon request in social situations, such as 'nice to see you' or 'thank you for coming'. Sometimes, with support, they may be able to recount experiences, show toys, say rhymes or sing songs to relatives or friends.

Adults should not feel that they must allow children to learn, copy or go on saying words or making sounds that make them feel uncomfortable or cross. Although all children encounter lavatorial humour, rude words, silly noises and laughing at situations that are not really funny, they can be immediately discouraged from continuing with them. It is perfectly acceptable for a home or early years setting not to allow certain words, noises or types of humour and children can learn and respect this from an early age, even if they are permitted to participate in different conversations in other places.

Many two year olds are already influenced by copying their peers within an early years setting or their siblings at home. This can mean that they learn undesirable ways to communicate at times, but ensures that they go on making the effort. Their play will still be mostly parallel at this stage, as they share toys and resources but create their own games alongside each other. However, cooperative play can often be achieved for short periods with the guidance and support of an adult who is playing with them.

At this age and stage, many children easily become upset or angry and cannot control their strong emotions, leading to tantrums and uncooperative behaviour. Adults should interpret children's behaviour by considering their abilities to verbalise and to understand the feelings and emotions they might have, the situations they are in and the relationships they rely upon. Behaviour is a core part of communication, along with verbal and non-verbal responses. Different behaviours can be indicators of areas of need.

Understanding development and behaviour

It is crucial that early years practitioners understand typical patterns of progress and are able to track the overall development of each child in their care. They are then able to offer advice and support to parents and other primary carers. Development of language helps children to understand what is happening around them, to make connections and to make their own needs and wishes known. If children struggle to develop language they will also have difficulty with forming social connections. Their frustrations and lack of ability to communicate their feelings can lead to behaviours such as hitting, pushing, pulling, grabbing, screaming, squealing and tantrums.

Adults need to recognise these behaviours as frustrations and ways of seeking attention, or as indicating a desire to join in with peers. Seen in this light, these negatively perceived behaviours can be observed as positive signs that children are interested in making relationships with others and becoming a part of the group. It is important to find the social intentions behind the undesirable actions and seek to help to decrease the frustrations, while supporting children in learning to use more acceptable methods of interaction.

Appreciating that the normal frustrations that can occur in everyday situations, which adults have already learned to deal with, can feel enormous to young children who are encountering them for the first time, can help to foster understanding, support and respect for the children's feelings. When instinctive reactions can be put aside and a teaching role assumed, children will learn how to react more positively on future occasions.

> A working mother is waiting at a doctor's surgery for a check up appointment with her son, Rupert, aged two and a half. The doctor is running late and she is beginning to worry about allowing time for the appointment before taking her son to his childminder and then getting to work at the time she promised, but she is trying to remain cheerful and enjoy the extra time with her son.
>
> Rupert asks her to read a story but she knows that they will be called at any moment. So, instead, she explains to Rupert that they don't have time to read a whole story now, but that they will ask his childminder to read his favourite story as soon as he arrives at her house and then they will choose two new books together to read at bedtime that night. She presents these ideas in an enthusiastic tone and asks him, 'Is that a good plan?'
>
> Rupert responds well to her positive attitude and agrees that they have made a good plan together. He then cooperates fully with the appointment and the journey to his childminder and is happy to say goodbye in time for his mother to leave for work, looking forward to the evening when she will return.

Avoiding the stresses of frustrations, arguments, whines, tears and upsets is not only happier for everybody, but saves a lot of time too. Talking things through and planning together builds strong and healthy relationships that will last. When they are unsure of what children want or why they are upset, adults should try taking what a child has said and rephrasing or rewording it before offering the sentence back to the child. Reflecting children's feelings and suggesting possible reasons for them can also help, as this proves to a child that their feelings are justified and acceptable, but that there may be better ways to express or deal with them that can be learned and the adult is willing to offer support in this.

For example, telling a child 'You say that you don't like your house any more because it looks horrible, but I think you're feeling angry because the glue is not strong enough to hold the pieces of your model together and disappointed that it fell over and doesn't look so good now', demonstrates that it's acceptable to mind when projects don't work out as planned. Going on to suggest ways of saving the model and supporting the child in carrying them out keeps adult and child firmly on the same side and working as a team within a positive relationship.

When requests do not work and instructions or commands lead to tantrums, carers could try singing instead of speaking them. It is possible to find and learn appropriate songs together that can be useful for defusing battles of wills in common situations such as meals, going out, going home, bath times and bed times. Some of these songs could come from the children's favourite CDs or DVDs and others could be traditional tunes with appropriate words substituted. Experienced practitioners will know that, when in doubt, *Here We Go Round The Mulberry Bush* usually works. The verse lyrics: 'This is the way we …' can cover most eventualities!

Singing develops listening and language skills and the control of the muscles of the mouth and throat. Carrying out instructions while singing them helps children to process and remember information. Also, using singing to get through unpopular and boring activities, especially as a group, is a good life strategy that has been used for hundreds of years.

Two year olds may surprise their families and carers with their mature perceptions at times, but amaze them with their vulnerability at others. At this age, children are unpredictable but they have an enormous capacity to grow, develop and influence those around them.

Enlarging the social circle
Two and a half years to three years

As children grow through the early years, ensuring effective communication becomes more and more important. Adults must send the messages that they want children to receive and work hard to ensure that they understand the signals the children are giving to them and interpret them correctly.

It is not good practice for children's caregivers to wonder what will happen each day and just cope with situations as they occur. This can lead to the same mistakes being made over and over again and adults becoming disillusioned and less confident, while children become frustrated, demanding and anxious.

Specific needs

Experienced carers should use their knowledge and experience of children at different stages of development to be aware of their needs and likely reactions. Parents and other relatives, who may be inexperienced in the care of young children, should observe them closely and learn about them as individuals, at the same time as seeking advice and support from those who can tell them more.

Practitioners have a responsibility to identify children who are failing to develop or struggling with speech, language or communication skills in the early years. Targeted help and support must be offered as early as possible in order to achieve better outcomes. Children receiving care from qualified early years practitioners may be identified as having Special Educational Needs or Disabilities (SEND) at any age, but communication needs are most often noticed between the ages of two and three years, when children are learning to speak or when they are settling into a pre-school or nursery class.

The 2014 *SEND Code of Practice* (page 79) states: 'All those who work with young children should be alert to emerging difficulties and respond early'. Early years practitioners will use their professional knowledge of child development, their experience of young children and their familiarity with the Early Years Foundation Stage (EYFS) to ensure that they are aware of potential and emerging difficulties.

They might notice that certain children are struggling to settle into a new group or environment, to join in with others, to understand routines or instructions or to express themselves. These children may not be able to answer questions, make choices, ask for what they need or request help. They may not understand how to participate when other children try to include them in their games or ask if they want to play. They might have little intelligible speech and be unable to say when they would like to join in or ask for a turn. They could be frustrated, which might make them aggressive, disruptive or upset. Or they might be afraid, bewildered, overwhelmed, quiet, passive or isolated.

If children are not progressing at the rate practitioners would predict when they consider the expected levels of development for their age group, or they are not achieving the EYFS early learning goals in the prime area of communication and language, extra help and support must be planned. Further advice from the 2014 *SEND Code of Practice* is that: 'Effective support for children with special educational needs should follow a graduated approach. Use an assess – plan – do review process to plan for, implement and review the support given'.

Observations can be used to assess all children's development and decide where their strengths lie, as well as which skills they need further support to develop. Children who find groups stimulating and are keen to play with others can be helped to learn to say the words and phrases that will encourage their peers to include them in their games. Those who concentrate for extended periods and create imaginative games and projects, but usually play alone, can be supported while they learn how to describe their ideas and how to invite friends to join them.

Describing their models and games to interested adults can encourage children to take their first steps towards inviting others into their play activities. Provided that genuine interest is shown and constructive questions are asked, children can feel rewarded for sharing their ideas and begin to believe that it might sometimes be more fun to play with a friend than to always play alone.

Two and a half years to three years

At the same time as extending the children's knowledge and understanding, adults may develop their social and communication skills through encouraging a new attitude to cooperative play, a desire to reach out to peers and the language and self-confidence with which to do so.

Figure 6.1 Discussing their models and games with others can help children to develop the skills needed for cooperative play.

Practitioners should talk with their key children's parents or main carers as soon as they suspect any emerging difficulties or identify a need for additional support. They can then decide together when it would be appropriate to speak to the Special Educational Needs Coordinator (SENCO) at the setting, and possibly other professionals, about how best to work with the children and any further help that may be available.

Initiating both informal discussions and more formal meetings with parents, carers, colleagues and specialists will enable practitioners to plan the support that will be offered to their key children. Each individual learning plan (ILP) must focus on the specific improvements that all of the relevant adults agree to be most desirable for that unique child. Following the plans will ensure that the help and support for each child can be implemented by practitioners within the setting, who are working consistently with the parents or carers at home.

Each key person should continue to record observations in the usual way and to assess children's responses based on this evidence. Meeting regularly with the other adults involved will allow the practitioners to discuss progress and determine how effective their help and support is proving to be. Looking back through observations and planned outcomes will show whether there is anything that should be added, removed or changed as time passes.

If further help or advice is required other professionals or specialists should be contacted and children may be assessed again with their support. It is essential to consider the individual needs of children, their whole families and any other primary carers at all times when planning to support delayed development of communication skills.

Good examples

As soon as children develop more fluent speech and are able to copy phrases and sentences, it is important for their primary caregivers to supply the words they would like them to use in typical situations, to set a good example at all times and to offer reminders, support and praise to motivate the children and encourage the desired behaviours.

Developing language skills allows children to link thoughts and make connections, gather information and explore new ideas, plan games, activities and projects, invite others to play, negotiate and problem solve. They can also speak confidently to adults to ask for what they need, to explain what they have achieved and what they are aiming to do next.

Research has proved that it is the children who, from an early age, are exposed to large amounts of language, extensive vocabularies and different types of speech who develop the ability to learn and use more words more quickly than those with less experience and encouragement. Young children do not find longer words harder to remember than shorter words and embrace new vocabulary to label and describe their interests, even when the words are not commonly used by most adults in their everyday lives.

Many two to three year olds love to learn and discuss the names of vehicles, machinery, animals or dinosaurs. They enjoy talking about an elevated platform truck and a pneumatic drill, or an armadillo and a dimetrodon, as much as a tractor or a crocodile. This is an ideal time to introduce children to the idea of looking up what they want to know, in order to find answers to questions, illustrations or more information on what they are interested in. Sharing books with pictures and diagrams, as well as accessing websites on tablets and computers, teaches children to be curious, to stay open-minded and interested in new ideas, to seek to increase their knowledge and understanding and to be proactive in finding out information for themselves as they grow older.

In typical development, the ability to use and understand language develops rapidly between the ages of two and three years, alongside greater social confidence, awareness of other children and cooperative play. Children begin to understand cause and effect, predict more accurately how their actions and responses might affect others and form friendships with peers. If children are not progressing as expected in the area of language development, practitioners must act to prevent them from becoming reliant upon negatively perceived behaviours, such as pushing, hitting or snatching, by offering other methods of communication.

> Maisie, aged two years and seven months, wants to play with her toy train on the floor, but sees her sister, Emily, aged ten months, crawling towards her to join in. Her instinctive reaction is to feel tense and to say 'Mine Emily!', while anticipating her sister grabbing for the train and spoiling the game.

Two and a half years to three years

But her mother has anticipated this stage as a potentially difficult time for the two girls to play together and is anxious to preserve their relationship, so she spends lots of time sitting with them while they play and explaining what is happening. Through this, Maisie knows that Emily cannot play carefully with her yet or talk about the game, but that she does not spoil games on purpose and that she will grow older and play nicely in the future. Maisie remembers and uses the strategies that her mother has modelled for her. She takes a figure from the train and holds it out to her sister, asking, 'Would Emily like one?'

The baby takes the figure with a smile and sits down to examine it. Maisie is now rewarded in three ways. She feels warm because her sister has smiled at her and is happy, she can play with her train without the baby touching it for at least two minutes and her mother praises her: 'That's very kind of you. She would like one. Thank you Maisie, that's lovely sharing. Aren't you lucky to have such a kind big sister, Emily?'

In order to continue the successful game and interactions, her mother now puts some animals in front of Emily and asks her: 'Can you share these with Maisie? Would Maisie like one? Could you give one to Maisie? Let's give one to Maisie and one to Emily. Now you can play together'.

When Emily tries to take a toy from Maisie, or Maisie wants a toy that Emily has, their mother expects Maisie to offer a swap or a distraction, rather than a fight or tears, or to ask an adult to intervene. When she remembers, she receives lots of praise and cuddles; when she does not quite manage it, her mother removes the source of conflict and then models the correct behaviour again. She also makes sure that Maisie has enough opportunities to play more complex games each day, uninterrupted by Emily, while the baby sleeps or plays separately.

It is important, when speaking to young children, to offer positive, constructive and specific advice and instructions. Telling or showing children exactly what they should do is more effective than asking them to 'be good'. Their perceptions of behaviour may differ hugely from that of adults, due to a lack of experience and conflicting needs and desires. Explaining that a sink will overflow if the water reaches the top is more valuable than forbidding children to put in the plug while the taps are running. Reminding them to put books back on the shelf is more friendly and likely to be obeyed than telling them not to leave books on the floor.

Children's curiosity is more powerful than their self control. At this young age, they are unlikely to remember previous accidents, make connections between similar incidents or predict potential mishaps when they are fascinated by something new. Their parents and carers can avoid upsets and help them to learn through exploring and investigating by demonstrating how to ask politely for what they would like to happen.

For example, if a child is offered a drink in a decorated cup with a water and glitter shaker sealed between two layers of clear plastic around the sides, the immediate reaction will be for the child to appreciate and explore the cup, turning and shaking it to find out what happens to the glitter and the pictures. Obviously, if the drink has already been poured, there is a high risk of it being spilled or tipped out, but a child will not think of that in their eagerness to explore. To avoid the inconvenience and upset of a spillage, a carer could ask on behalf of the child, 'That is such a wonderful cup, could we please look at it first and see how it works?'

While the cup is empty, the child can tilt and shake it or hold it upside down to explore the patterns it makes and talk about it with the adults. After curiosity has been satisfied, the child can be given a drink and asked to hold the cup carefully. If it is not possible to ask in advance, because the liquid has already been poured out, the adult could remind the child to be careful at first but promise that, once the drink has been finished, the empty cup may be explored and examined in detail. It may be necessary to offer praise and support at intervals to prevent frustration and encourage patience.

Rising threes should be encouraged to state politely what they would like to do and, as far as possible, to explain why. This will usually demonstrate to adults that their intentions are good and their behaviour not deliberately bad, but that it is their inexperience or impulsiveness that leads to accidents or misunderstandings.

The same principle applies to praise and criticism. Remarking upon careful cutting out, concentration during a game or kindness in sharing with a friend is more useful and likely to encourage repetition than a bland 'well done' or 'thank you'. Explaining why it was unfair to spoil a game or dangerous to jump too close to other children promotes understanding rather than resentment.

Two and a half years to three years

Conversations and chatting

Children aged between two and a half and three years are often very chatty. They are delighting in their now confident ability to express themselves, they are interested in everything around them and they have a lot to say. They may talk to themselves and their toys, as well as to friends, siblings and adults, especially while deeply absorbed in play. This helps them to order and develop their thoughts and practise new vocabulary and sentence structure.

Parents, other family members and primary carers can introduce new ideas and characters to their children by initiating or joining in with imaginative games. Two year olds love role play involving dolls or soft toys and are stimulated and excited when adults make the toys talk, especially in a variety of different voices. They do know that the toys are not really speaking, but enjoy suspending disbelief for the duration of a game. Favourite games often involve meals, picnics and parties or going to sleep and waking up.

Less familiar experiences, such as dolls using a lift while shopping or teddies going on a train journey, can fascinate children aged between two and a half and three years. They may listen in wonder while a role play game unfolds and, when it ends, say 'Tell me that again!'

They cannot immediately reproduce the game without help, but they want to repeat the pleasurable experience and learn to do so through repetition. Adults must understand that opportunities to repeat the same games are important and be patient enough to lead, or at least begin, the same imaginative experiences many times, until the children are able to take the games and make them their own. Young children re-enact favourite role plays and stories to memorise them for pleasure, in the same way that adults listen to the same favourite songs or pieces of music many times until they learn them by heart.

Small world characters can be invaluable when adults want to recreate scenarios for or with children. They are attractive to handle and easily inspire imagination.

While playing out favourite scenes with children and encouraging them to join in, adults may model appropriate language, responses and manners or demonstrate what could happen if a character behaved badly or forgot to be careful or sensible. Children are more likely to learn, understand and remember morals, manners and sensitivity towards others if these values are communicated to them through stories.

Two and a half years to three years

Figure 6.2 People of all ages find that attractive or realistic small world characters can inspire imaginative games.

Adults living or working with children of this age should make a habit of speaking just slightly more slowly, clearly, politely and correctly than they usually would with their own family, as though they are teaching a class or visiting relatives that they do not see very often. If this is the type of speech that young children most usually hear while they are developing language skills it will be what they copy, ensuring that their basic speech will be polite and correct and that it will be pleasant for others to listen to and converse with them. Relying upon this firm foundation, they will be able to automatically adapt their speech to suit different people and situations as they grow older, but will remain intelligible and in control when anxious or under stress.

Once they feel confident enough in any situation, children of this age are usually prepared to speak and should be intelligible to strangers who are prepared to listen carefully enough. If developing as expected, their speech will now make full use of digraphs and trigraphs, which are the combined sounds such as 'sh', 'ch', 'th' and 'scr', 'spl', 'thr'. The more difficult single sounds, such as 'r' and 'y', will usually now be corrected too, although some children will take a little longer to master these. Mistakes made with a few of these sounds, occasional confusions or mix-ups need not be a cause for concern at this stage, provided confident communication and understanding is possible and children are happy to talk.

Cooperation and performing to others

At this age children can become aware of being a member of a group, if they attend an early years setting or social groups with a parent or carer or have friends to play at home. They will begin to understand how to play cooperatively with other children and sometimes enjoy doing so. They will respond to group activities, such as action songs, stories, crafts, baking or chasing games in the garden, when these are led by a strong, sensitive and inspiring practitioner. Making music, dancing and singing may become very popular and children will develop a greater repertoire and begin to sing and dance on their own, sometimes performing to a group of peers or to family members.

When appropriate, adults may organise short, fairly informal shows with the children who attend an early years setting or a private music, dance or drama group and help them to perform to their own families, friends and carers. These may involve dressing up and speaking to the audience, along with group songs, mimes and movements, and can provide enormous boosts to the confidence and self-esteem of those children who enjoy them, as well as memories to share and treasure together as a group.

The ability to stand up and speak to a group when they have something to say, or to deliver a prepared speech or presentation, or to perform a song or a dance for an audience are all important communication tools that may be valuable or essential in later life. The purpose of any kind of performance is to inspire, inform or entertain. People should be empowered from early childhood to develop the skills to do this for themselves and for others.

Some children do continue to enjoy spending time alone, engaged in solitary play, and this should not be discouraged, provided that they do join in with their peers at other times. Others only play alone because they do not know how to join a group. It is important to get to know children well as individuals, to be sure of their preferences and then to respect them.

When a practitioner in a setting thinks that a key child is just beginning to move out of the solitary play stage and would welcome some company, a good starting point is for various adults to ask whether they can sit with the child to play or chat for a few minutes at a time. Colleagues can be asked to

Two and a half years to three years

Figure 6.3 Speaking and performing to others can boost confidence and self-esteem and enable children to develop skills that will be valuable in later life.

help with this. It will then be possible to gradually encourage other children who have shared interests or similar personalities to join the child one at a time and then to invite the child to join them in a small group.

Copying another child or doing as the others in the group are doing is a way of communicating that they would now like to fit in and be included, and is an early way of making friends. They may understand each other's needs more easily than adults and offer interesting insights if asked for ideas on alternative ways to achieve aims.

When introducing a new story book for the first time to a two year old, an adult must try to ensure that it is read to an individual child or a very small group. Time must be taken to explore the words and pictures and to savour the rhythm and any alliteration or rhymes.

If the story is a success, the child will immediately ask for it to be read again. The adult should repeat the story exactly as before, allowing the child time to assimilate the information and the ideas and to memorise the characters and the structure of the story. In further readings the adult can begin to pause before some key words and the words at the ends of lines or sentences, using inflections, emphasis, pictures and actions to encourage the child to speak them on cue, alone or in unison with others in the group. With practice, the child's ability and confidence in this area will gradually increase, until many favourite stories are known by heart and can be recited using the pictures in the books as a guide. These are important skills to develop before beginning to learn to read.

Developing vocabulary and memories

Very young children have limited vocabularies with which to express all that they want to say. Teachers of secondary school students who are learning a new language know that sometimes the writing on the page appears to be nonsense at first, but translating literally what has been said makes the intention clear and they are then able to supply the correct words to create the sentence. In the same way, if a young child's statement sounds incorrect to an adult, it is worth considering carefully what was said and thinking literally, as a simple rephrasing may make the meaning clear and reveal a true understanding of a situation.

For example, a child may state that he has two nurseries and one Grandma now, but that, when he grows older, he will have lots of schools. A parent or practitioner listening only to his words will tell him that actually he has two Grandmas but only one nursery and that he will go on to attend just one school at a time. However, a carer who is truly tuned in to this child's thinking and understanding will be able to see the situation in the way he does and accept his choice of words as representative of his thoughts, explaining for him: 'You mean that you go to nursery on two days each week and spend one day with Grandma, but, when you're big enough to go to school, you'll go there on five days each week'.

Rising threes have lots of questions and ask about everything that fascinates them. Adults should try to give clear and simple answers and encourage them to make connections within their own experiences and build on what they already know.

If a child asks, 'Why is juice wet?' the reply might be, 'The fruit is mixed with water. All drinks are made with water and water is always wet, whether it comes from the taps or from the rain outside'.

The answer to 'How can I build a very tall tower?' might be, 'Try putting the biggest and heaviest bricks at the bottom to make it strong and balancing

Two and a half years to three years

the smaller ones carefully on top. Remember how the heavy ones fall and knock the others down if you don't use them first'.

It is easier to cement children's understanding of important basic concepts by focusing on them one at a time. In a setting, using themed stories, posters and collections on tables or inviting children to bring in relevant items for 'show and tell' circle or group times can involve families in their children's learning. When one or two concepts are focused on during each day or week, such as colours, shapes, numbers, animals, vehicles or places, it should be possible for groups to explore many themes and for adults and children to find references all around them.

Thomas, aged two years and six months, plays with a new toy and suddenly says, 'This puzzle is from Auntie Deborah. It came in a big box. Mummy opened it with scissors'. His mother replies, 'You're right. Auntie Deborah brought this puzzle for you when she came to see us last week, didn't she? And the box was stuck with tape, so we had to cut it open carefully, so that we didn't tear the picture. Well remembered, Thomas!'

At teatime, Thomas eats some cake and says, 'I made cake with Daddy'.

His mother says, 'Yes, you and Daddy made this cake yesterday, didn't you? You were clever. Are you enjoying it? Thank you for letting me have some'.

Thomas sees the grazes on his knees when he gets undressed at bed time and says, 'I chased Grandpa. I fell over. Hurt my knees on the path'. His mother replies, 'Yes, you were having such a lovely game playing outside with Grandpa. It was a shame when you fell and bumped your knees, but they're nearly better now'.

Memory capacity increases in children over two and half years and they begin to develop the ability to call memories to mind at appropriate times. They do not yet have the control to recall memories at will, but will have flashes of vivid recollection when reminded of an interesting, enjoyable or dramatic event by a visual or aural clue.

Children may now be able to remember the games and activities that they have participated in and describe them to parents and other carers later. They may tell their nanny or childminder during the afternoon about a story at pre-school that morning, or talk with their mother or father at bedtime about a trip to the park in the afternoon. These memories cannot yet be easily called to mind, but occur spontaneously and must be verbalised immediately or temporarily lost again. Adults should avoid asking too many questions and confusing children or making them search for correct answers, but be prepared to wait and always show interest when they do remember events and choose to share them.

Although children of this age do not deliberately make jokes, they can be very funny. As long as they feel that their families or carers are laughing with them, rather than at them, they love to amuse people and appreciate the warm feeling gained from enjoying a shared joke together.

Parents may frequently ask their children to play together and to allow siblings to join in with games or take turns with favourite toys, telling them that: 'It's called sharing'. They should not be surprised if two to three year olds who choose to take a forbidden item and give it to a doll or teddy, or to give toys to a sibling to avoid having to tidy them away, then repeat the phrase: 'It's called sharing' when challenged. They are not being deliberately awkward, but just interpreting literally a concept that they are trying to understand. A sense of humour helps at these times! The difficult but important task for the adults is to see and share the joke, but to firmly guide the children to learn when it is appropriate to use the phrase, while maintaining close and respectful relationships with them.

By the age of three, children will be able to form clear ideas of what they would like to achieve and what they want from other people. They will try to explain, but some of their ideas may not be possible or intelligible, which can lead to further frustrations. However, they should now be moving towards a stage of greater understanding and reason. If adults speak and listen to them respectfully and treat them fairly, they will usually be able to understand the reasons why they cannot do or have certain things, or why they must wait, share, take turns or compromise.

Children need lots of support at this age to consolidate their abilities in understanding and accepting postponement of gratification. They are also beginning to understand bargains and working for rewards. Successful conversations might now include, 'You go and choose some books while I put the baby to bed and then, while he's asleep, we'll read stories together' and

'When we've finished tidying up the kitchen and our biscuits are ready to come out of the oven, we can have a drink and a snack'.

Non-verbal communication, music and rhythm

Children with special or additional needs or disabilities may need to communicate in alternative ways and may be less able to express themselves, but must be encouraged to do so and supported in all the attempts they make. Sometimes, children will need to make enormous efforts to send a simple message or response and this effort must be appreciated and rewarded. If they do not receive the gratification of their needs or wishes, appropriate attention and sufficient praise or comfort, these children may stop making the effort to communicate and become isolated and unhappy, which will also have a negative impact upon their development and daily life. When children are working hard to communicate, adults must also work hard to offer them the best possible care.

> Sally, aged two years and eleven months, has profound disabilities and extremely complex needs. She is unable to speak or walk and does not have enough control of her arm movements to use signs or point to pictures. However, she is able to use her face expressively and to make deliberate movements with her eyes and her head.
>
> She wears a red band on her left wrist, which she looks at when she would like food or a drink, and a blue band on her right wrist, which she looks at when she needs to have her nappy changed or help with another personal care routine. If she is asked appropriate questions, Sally can hold her head up and smile to indicate 'yes' or drop her head down and make a cross face for 'no'.
>
> Her parents and her learning support assistant at her nursery watch her attentively to ensure that they do not miss any of the signals that she gives, and have become adept in obtaining information through asking questions that require only 'yes' and 'no' answers. They are confident that Sally is comfortable with this and not frustrated so far, but plan to introduce more advanced methods of communication gradually as she grows older.

Two and a half years to three years

It is important always to remember that, while speech and language are an important part of our culture, it is not the only form of communication. Humans have been communicating with each other since they first evolved, before the development of speech, and people who speak are also able to converse with those who use other languages and those who are deaf or mute. Animals send messages to those of their own species and others. Humans and animals also communicate with each other.

If children are struggling with speech and language skills, or unable to develop them, adults must find another way to communicate. It may be necessary to be inventive, ingenious or unorthodox, but it is vital to unlock children's silent worlds and welcome them into a place where they may make decisions, express opinions and share ideas.

> Atte, aged three years, has come from Finland to live in England with his family and has recently started to attend an English pre-school. He has quickly learned that the other children and staff do not understand the words he uses when he speaks in Finnish, but he is a naturally talkative child and so is eager to be able to chat in English. He works hard to learn new words every day, listens carefully to stories and discussions and tries out the phrases he hears. Practitioners are keen to help Atte to feel confident in his use of the second language and are willing to chat with him whenever he wants to. His key person recognises that he is a very intelligent child, who learns quickly and wants to get things right, so she works with him on correct sentence structure and word order each day, using games, stories, songs and rhymes.
>
> Soon, Atte shares his English words at home and often translates for his mother, who is also learning English. Upon arrival in the mornings he speaks Finnish with his mother, but remembers to greet the staff and children in English. When she collects him at lunchtimes he speaks English at first, but reverts to his first language as they leave the building.
>
> Atte's key person encourages him to tell the group some key words in Finnish during circle times and they all practise saying them. Eventually, he is able to teach them a Finnish song and his mother comes into the setting to help everybody to sing it. The other children are excited to be able to speak and sing in a new language.

Two and a half years to three years

When a family from another country enters an early years setting it is important to make the most of the opportunity to learn about their language and culture, as well as to share the setting's language and culture with them. Staff should be confident and inventive in finding alternative ways to communicate with children and their families while they help them to gradually develop skills in the language of the setting, but should also prepared to learn and use new languages themselves whenever appropriate. All practitioners, children and families may benefit from exploring and embracing diversity in this way.

Music and rhythm is a universal language that can bring people together. It can also help children to develop language and communication skills in an enjoyable way. In an early years setting practitioners will use games with percussion instruments to support children as they learn to listen to and recognise different sounds, beats and rhythms. Parents and carers can encourage these developing abilities at home too, using instruments or homemade drums, rattles and shakers.

Figure 6.4 Music and rhythm is a universal language and children can use percussion instruments to learn about sounds and beats.

Two and a half years to three years

Understanding separate sounds and beats helps children to create ordered speech, without muddles, and to speak at an appropriate pace, without leaving unusual pauses or rushing to complete sentences. A sense of rhythm enables children to take note of intonations and inflections within the language that they speak and to reproduce them naturally, so that they may ask questions, express feelings and maintain the interest of their listeners.

Using percussion instruments or homemade drums and shakers to play along to nursery rhymes and songs is a very valuable activity. Listening to different beats helps children to hear and differentiate between sounds, while moving objects in time to a beat develops coordination. These are important skills that will aid clear speech and, later, learning to read. Making sounds of different kinds helps children to express themselves confidently.

Reading and writing

Before the age of three years some children will be interested in printed words and try to follow them in books as they sit close to a family member or carer to listen to readings of information texts, stories and rhymes. They will also ask for words to be written to describe their drawings, models and paintings and attempt to write some letters and words for themselves. They will make shapes and squiggles in lines with spaces between them which, at first glance, could be taken for a genuine text in a language unfamiliar to the reader. For others, this stage will come later.

Whether children are under three or over five, or anywhere in between, it is vital that they are supported and encouraged when they first display an interest in reading and writing, and that their early attempts at remembering, guessing and deciphering words and creating emergent writing are valued and built upon.

Providing a range of books, magazines, comics, posters, scrapbooks and photograph albums and an extensive choice of papers and cards, pens, pencils and paints, as well as a blackboard with chalks, wipe clean surfaces and opportunities to make marks in sand, mud and other substances, both indoors and outside, will allow children to develop skills at their own pace during this important stage. Adults should ensure that they are good role models, demonstrating the usefulness and the pleasure of creating, absorbing, using and enjoying words and pictures.

Two and a half years to three years

Figure 6.5 Children will begin to use emergent writing if they have a range of opportunities and resources to make marks when they are ready.

Routines and instructions

Routines within a setting can go smoothly if expectations are realistic and if children understand what is asked of them. If they do not, practitioners must consider what has been heard by the children and rephrase instructions in words they will more easily understand. For example, 'We must tidy up the toys now because it will soon be time to go home. Please stop playing and work together to put everything back in its place'.

Younger children need a specific instruction and then help, support and praise to enable them to carry out the task. Adults should avoid muddling or distracting them with additions such as, 'Do it nicely. Stack the bricks properly. Share the broom'.

To extend language further, it is better for adults to talk to children individually while working alongside small groups. For example, 'Let's put the pens into the box first. Could you please pick up those two pens from the floor? Could you please pass me the lid for the box? Shall we put this paper into the drawer now? Let's fold up the tablecloth and put it into the cupboard'.

This approach will be standard practice within a high quality early years setting. Many of these principles may be applied at home with equal success.

Finding a place
Three years to three and a half years

From the age of three years, children become more sociable and interested in other people. Although some may be shy, quiet or less confident in new situations, most will speak and listen within a familiar group and may often be influenced by others enough to copy ideas and behaviour. This can be very positive for the development of understanding, negotiation and group work skills, but can be less positive when children copy less desirable behaviours and silly words or actions, or make each other too excited or distracted to cope. Natural leaders may begin to emerge from this young age and experienced early years practitioners will recognise them within a group.

> Amiya, aged three years and one month, walks confidently into the doctor's waiting room with her father. She looks around at the room and obviously remembers the place from previous visits. She asks her father, 'Are we going upstairs?' When he says that today they are not, she says, 'Stay here then' and walks purposefully over to the toy boxes, singing to herself. After exploring the crayons, books and rocking horse, she notices the large clock on the wall and stands in front of it, saying loudly, 'Excuse me, clock!' several times. Amiya then looks around at the other people in the waiting room, sees that some of them are smiling at her and gives a little spin on the spot.
>
> She looks at each person in turn, trying to make eye contact and smiling, to see whether they will return the smile. One or two smile but then look away, while others read magazines and do not look directly at her. One lady smiles warmly, inviting further interaction.

Three years to three and a half years

> Amiya immediately recognises that this is a person who might enjoy speaking and playing with her. She fetches the empty crayon box and asks, 'Shall I balance this on my head?' With encouragement she manages to do this, but it is obvious that her real desire is the stimulation of initiating and holding a conversation with a new person, with the security of her father's presence in the background.

Social interactions

Three year olds may make overtures towards other people, even strangers, because they enjoy social interactions and would rather initiate them than play alone or be ignored. They may communicate with new people through smiles and other expressions, gestures and actions before using speech.

When meeting a three year old for the first time, an adult can expect that the child may feel shy, nervous or apprehensive and should try to make the first conversations as natural and positive as possible. Some children are self-confident and extrovert by nature, while others are quieter or less vocal by choice, but many will be unsure during early interactions with unfamiliar people, then warm up and become chatty once they feel at ease in the situation.

The same strategies may be employed for all children, but the patience required while waiting for their responses will differ according to individual children's personalities and previous experiences. Family friends, relatives, nannies or childminders who are meeting children that they have been asked to care for should aim to be friendly and welcoming, confident and interesting and speak to the children at an appropriate level. This means squatting down to achieve eye contact, greeting the children by name and introducing themselves. It is a good idea to follow this immediately with a question such as: 'Would you like to come and play at my house? I've got trains, a garage and cars, a dolls' house, bricks and playdough' or 'I'm sure you've got some good toys to show me at your house and perhaps we could do some baking or make a model'.

When children respond in any way, however small, the adults can begin to build relationships by talking about their favourite toys or activities, answering their questions or reassuring them if they have any worries. Sometimes parents are

Three years to three and a half years

Figure 7.1 Toys, games and activities can be adapted flexibly to suit different levels of development.

astonished at how quickly their previously timid or reserved children will begin to talk to caring adults who approach them with confidence and experience.

Creative use of resources

Young children will often wish to play with toys more suitable for older ones and adapt toys, games and activities to suit their own levels of development. This flexibility and critical and creative thinking must be encouraged, as the ability to use resources appropriately in different situations, and not to be limited to prescribed, obvious or already established ideas, is a skill shared by those who lead and succeed as adults.

Very few resources cannot be used in some way by young children where there is careful supervision and where adequate help and guidance are provided when necessary. It is good practice to offer the philosophy that anybody can use what they have to make things happen and to fulfil the purposes and ideas that they choose.

Practitioners working in an early years setting can use a similar strategy when greeting visiting children or settling new children into the nursery,

85

pre-school or crèche. Welcoming children and their parents or carers by inviting them to join in with activities or choose toys is less threatening to nervous children than walking around, looking at things or talking.

After a parent or carer leaves a child, an experienced practitioner will know that remaining physically close for a while is important to the newly settling child and offers opportunities for a bond to be formed between child and key person, as it communicates the feeling that this adult is now there for the child and will ensure safety, comfort, listening, encouragement, support, interesting challenges and lots of fun.

Language development and thinking skills can be especially encouraged and promoted in children between three years and three and a half years through the sharing of stories, songs and rhymes and engaging in discussions and imaginative flights of fantasy.

Constructive conversations

Children naturally gravitate towards adults who demonstrate interests that they share, as well as towards other children who like to play with the same toys or in the same areas. For example, the children in a setting who are fascinated by dinosaurs will ask for the toys and then seek out the practitioner who confidently names and describes them and enjoys discussing their features and habits. The practitioner can use these conversations as opportunities to extend play and to model, teach and encourage communication and social skills, logic, reasoning and creative thinking, as well as imparting knowledge, facts and imagination.

An example of such a constructive conversation between an adult and a child might be:

'What's this one called?'
'It's a stegosaurus. You can recognise it by the line of spikes on its back. They protect it from other dinosaurs who might try to eat it. It's a plant eater and it has to protect itself from the meat eaters by being too hard for them to bite.'
'Some of the other ones have spikes.'
'Yes, some other dinosaurs have spikes too, but they look different. This one's an ankylosurus, with spikes all over its back and at the end of its tail. This is a sailback lizard and its real name is dimetrodon.'

'I like the stegosaurus. And I like this one, but it's fierce. I know it's the tyrannosaurus and it's a meat eater, so it eats the other dinosaurs.'

'Yes, it's very fierce, isn't it? Is that one your favourite? My favourite is the triceratops because I love its three horns.'

'I like that triceratops too. But it's not as fierce as my tyrannosaurus with all the sharp teeth and the big tail.'

'No, you're right, it's not. Shall we make them a place to live? What sort of homes might they like to have?'

Observing children engaging in role play, puppet play, small world play or artwork can be enormously valuable at this age, as it can show adults what happens in children's lives. They will naturally imitate and reproduce the experiences they have had, as well as stories that they know, which can help carers to understand why they do or think certain things. When children are dressing up as characters within their own families and acting out or talking about what happens at home, at a relative's house or in another setting, practitioners in an early years setting can find out more details of the children's home lives and may come to understand parents' attitudes, policies and behaviour management or the customs of other cultures more clearly.

At times, this can enable children to demonstrate previously undiscovered areas of knowledge and competence; at other times it can be a cry for help, when children cannot or dare not tell of abuse or talk about unhappy experiences more directly.

It is also possible to impart information about various occupations and situations to children through acting out characters in role play and imaginative games. If adults take turns to become different people, they can effectively model character acting, showing children how to play in this way and how to talk to each other in role, while exploring facts and details. Some children will naturally understand and imitate this type of play, but others will need to be encouraged to express themselves imaginatively, to create and follow their own ideas or to cooperate within a group.

In exploratory and discovery play, small world or construction play or arts and crafts, adults should sit down with children and listen to their conversations before joining in. They should aim to be play partners and not teachers, avoiding dominating the situation by asking too many questions or directing the areas to be discussed, but adding small extensions to the children's creative stories, ideas and theories without seeking to change them.

Three years to three and a half years

Comparing different objects with the same name, such as a collection of spoons made from metal, wood, rubber and plastic in various colours and sizes, or toy cars representing a variety of makes and models, or pictures of many breeds of dog, can help children to understand that language contains both general and more specific labels for larger groups and smaller sub-sets.

Matching and describing different objects that are the same colour, or are made from the same material, or perform the same function, is a useful activity that helps children to link and order their ideas and learn to use words to describe more abstract concepts.

Knowing that 'spoon' refers to the shape and function of an object, but not its colour or texture, while 'green' can describe any item with a particular appearance and 'heavy' labels how an object feels but not what it looks like, demonstrates a level of language maturity that can be reached by three year olds who have been exposed to an environment rich in opportunities for quality speech and language learning. They are already beginning to distinguish between nouns, verbs and adjectives without knowing that they are doing so.

Figure 7.2 Comparing objects can give children an understanding of materials, functions and abstract concepts.

Three years to three and a half years

Visual impairment

Children who are blind or visually impaired are usually able to develop speech and language skills without difficulty, but they do not have the stimulus that makes them want to talk when they cannot see what is around them. The concepts of size, shape, weight and texture become more important and giving them the words to describe these is vital. It is necessary for those caring for these children to share the richness of language and give them the gift of imagination, as well as the ability to use clues to interpret what they sense and feel. If adults set a good example, children can absorb the best way to speak to siblings and friends with visual impairments from a young age.

> Lily, aged three years and three months, attends a crèche with her brother, Tarell, aged four years and five months. Tarell is visually impaired and can see only shapes and shades of light and dark. The children have not been to the crèche before, but their mother is confident that they will be fine because Lily is prepared to look after Tarell and play with him and she will interpret his needs well enough to explain to an adult if he becomes upset or needs to go to the toilet.
>
> As they enter the play area, Lily walks beside Tarell, holding his hand and looking all around her. She immediately begins to talk, clearly and continuously, as though she is 'seeing' for Tarell: 'Oh, they've got some bricks like ours - the ones that feel smooth - do you want to touch them? Let's sit down here. It's a soft mat. The marbles are here. I'll help you put them in the top of the run. Can you hear them rattling down? Put your hand here and you can feel them at the bottom and pick them up again. Stand up now and we'll go to the table because there's playdough. Hold my hand. It's this way, Forward four steps, no, two more. Now here's a chair. Feel the back of it and there's the seat part. Here's the table. Put your hand on it and you can find how to sit down. Here's some playdough for you and I've got some. Shall we roll some long snakes? It feels nice, doesn't it?'
>
> Throughout this monologue, Tarell does as Lily says, smiling as he feels the bricks, the marbles and the playdough and saying 'Yes' several times. Once he is seated at the table and enjoying the texture of the

Three years to three and a half years

> playdough between his fingers, he feels confident enough to start to chat with Lily about what they might make.
>
> Another child approaches the table and Lily immediately says, 'Hello, do you like playdough too? Do you want to join in with us? I'm Lily and this is my brother, Tarell. He can't see like us, but he can talk and he's good at making things'.

If children live with siblings who are visually impaired they will understand them as individuals and simply accept their disabilities as a part of who they are. If parents and other adults model and demonstrate how to care for the children and how to speak to them, siblings may often be prepared to follow these examples and temporarily take on the responsibility of staying with them and interpreting for them in certain situations. Provided that this does not happen too often and that young children do not feel under pressure to assume full responsibility for their sibling's needs and wellbeing, it can be very valuable for their relationships with their brothers and sisters and for their understanding of tolerance and diversity.

Children with visual impairments will feel most confident when they hear clear instructions about where they are and what they are likely to encounter. Descriptions of toys and equipment, directions and numbers of steps to furniture and doors and explanations of people present will help in unfamiliar situations. They should be invited to touch and feel items such as tables and chairs or bathroom fixtures, in order to form an idea within their mind of their placements and sizes, so that they may use them safely.

There is no value in talking about colours or shapes to children who cannot see them or distinguish between them. Textures are of more interest to them and they may be invited to touch items and surfaces to discuss whether they are rough or smooth, hard or soft, pointed or flat. Their emphasis will always be on what they can feel, so they will prefer to play with malleable materials, craft activities and construction kits. Mixing paint colours will be of no interest, but finger painting or handprints could be enjoyable. Learning to recognise tiny differences between the things they touch will be invaluable if they are likely to go on to learn to read Braille as they grow older.

Depending on the degree of visual impairment, large picture books, friezes and posters or black and white patterns and symbolic pictures may have some value and help with the acquisition of vocabulary. Stories and rhymes, singing and making music should form an important part of these children's lives and can encourage them to join in with group activities to develop language and understanding skills and relationships with their peers. A specialist professional will be able to offer more useful information and advice to parents or early years staff.

Taking cues

Children enjoy supplying missing words or alternating phrases when an adult pauses in the reading or telling of a story or rhyme, and taking cues in this way increases general awareness and logical thinking. It is also a useful skill to practise and will help children throughout their primary school years and beyond, when they are called upon to take part in performances and classroom discussions.

Adults can initiate this activity using books and rhymes that the children already know well, then move on to trying it with less familiar ones. Some three year olds will not understand immediately but, over a period of a few months, most will grasp the idea and find the challenge stimulating. It can also be a useful method of checking understanding, attitude and progress.

If an adult says, 'One little speckled frog sat on a speckled - ?' a child who has achieved full understanding of the game will reply 'log'. An imaginative child, who understands rhyme but is less concerned, so far, about the words making sense, may try 'fog' or 'jog'. A logically thinking child, who pays more attention to meaning than to the way words sound or flow, might offer 'rock' or 'lily pad'. Children who do not yet understand may not spontaneously reply when the pause comes. If prompted, they may say any word, such as 'house' or 'green', or even just repeat 'frog', especially if there is a picture or another visual clue. These children need more support, repetition and opportunities to practise and play with words.

Tact and manners

Some three year olds can sound rude or tactless when speaking to adults, when they are actually just trying to find out a piece of information that is important to them. They may use the only words they know to say what they mean, rather than choosing the politer form more often used in social situations that is, as yet, outside their experience.

For example, a child might turn to a favourite relative or friend soon after they arrive and ask, 'When are you going?' This, of course, sounds at first as though they are hoping that the person will leave soon when, in fact, the opposite is true and they are seeking reassurance that they will have plenty of time to enjoy the visit. A parent or nanny must be prepared to explain quickly, 'What you really mean to say is – how long can you stay?' Social conventions are not all absorbed by the age of three.

> Yusuf, aged three years and five months, watches his sister, Yasmin, aged two years, colouring wildly all over a sheet of paper and waits patiently for two minutes. When she shows no signs of stopping, he says, 'I need the red pen now, Yasmin'.
>
> When Yasmin does not respond, Yusuf tries again, 'Please can I have the red pen now? I think it is my turn'.
>
> Still not achieving the desired result, Yusuf remembers and tries a different method that he has been shown at pre-school. He picks up a pink pen and an orange pen and offers them to Yasmin, asking, 'Would you like one of these pens now, to make your picture really nice?'
>
> Yasmin smiles and takes the pink pen, putting the red one down on the table. She begins to make pink marks on top of her red ones. Yusuf smiles and says, 'Thank you', taking the red pen and returning to his own drawing.

Children over three years can understand, learn and remember how to use some basic good manners and how to persuade others to share and take turns without conflict or power struggles. If adults model the language they would like to hear through their own speech and supply words at appropriate moments to encourage children, there is a good chance that they will be copied. If children regularly hear mothers say, 'Could you give me the book, please?' or fathers say, 'Thank you for tidying up the bricks', they are more likely to ask their siblings, 'Can it be my turn next, please?' and 'Thank you for sharing the pencils'.

When practitioners in early years settings ask children, 'Please could everybody wash their hands and sit down?' and say, 'Thank you for putting on your coats and shoes sensibly so that we can have lots of time to play outside', they are likely to be more successful in persuading the children to ask, 'Please may I have a drink?' and to say, 'Thank you for helping me'.

Children who forget to ask politely, when they are able to do so, can be gently prompted and encouraged to copy the appropriate words. Adults who hear, 'Can I have one?' should reply, 'Please. Yes, you may have one' and pass the desired items. If children try to take objects but forget to acknowledge the giver, the adults should hold on for just a moment longer than usual and say 'Thank you' on their behalf before releasing the objects.

It is important for those who care for other people's children to remember that languages and cultures differ in their uses and expectations of manners. Some children will not have experience of words such as 'please' and 'thank you' in their first languages and will not use them with their families at home, so they may encounter them for the first time when they begin to attend an early years setting and will need extra time and support to allow them to master this concept. However, it is important that they do learn to use the social customs of the country in which they live and to understand that these words matter to the people around them.

It is important to create and manage routines for young children, within an early years setting or a home, by using consistent language and phrases in the same order every day. Practitioners, parents or other carers must listen to each other and ensure that they are clear in their intentions and in reinforcing their expectations, rather than giving out confused or mixed messages. Children can cope with different routines, activities, people, food and even languages in different situations, as long as each is consistent within itself, but they cannot be expected to manage widely differing expectations in the areas of behaviour or independence.

An example of clear and specific instructions that sound firm but friendly and encourage small children to comply might be:

'It's time for lunch. Please go to wash your hands and then come and sit at your table. Use your fork or your spoon to eat your food, but not your hands. You can talk quietly with your friends, but please don't shout. Sit still on your chair until you've had enough to eat and then you may ask to leave the table. We don't stand up or walk around while we're eating our lunch'.

Practitioners in a setting must be aware that some children may never have experienced meals in this way at home and they may feel anxious or confused at first, but they are able to learn a new set of behaviours to use within a new situation. If the adults remain consistent and firm but understanding

Three years to three and a half years

and supportive, most children will conform and others will copy and learn from them. Those who struggle to understand, remember or cooperate must receive one-to-one support while they learn not to disrupt the routine and atmosphere for the group.

Excitement can make all children restless and boredom can make them lethargic or keen to find mischief. They may achieve less or regress if they feel worried or under pressure to perform or behave in a way that is unnatural or beyond their capabilities. They may need extra comfort or over-react to sensory stimuli if they are tired or hungry or coping with difficult experiences at home. Carers should aim, wherever possible, to provide an environment in which all children can feel happy, interested and stimulated, but also calm, confident and in control. Rhythmic physical activities, such as jumping, clapping, banging a drum or bouncing on a trampoline, can often help more exuberant children or those with less coordination who need support to find a calm, steady pace.

There will be incidents when three year olds try to use their newly acquired manners to reinforce their refusals of some suggestions or instructions. They will need to learn through experience that saying 'No, thank you' very politely is not enough to ensure that they can miss meal times, bath times, bed times or getting ready to go out, and that saying 'Please may I have it?' will not always guarantee them receiving whatever they desire. Parents and carers need to explain that some requests are not really choices or optional decisions at all, but that asking 'Would you like to?' sounds so much more polite and friendly than 'You have to!'

Children will gradually learn to recognise which questions are choices and which are non-optional requests and, hopefully, begin to speak politely to others in the same way. But this will not stop them from refusing to comply whenever they are not in the right mood.

There will also be times when children feel unable to share or allow others to take a turn because the possession is too precious or their game would be spoiled. At these times, it is important that they are able to say calmly 'I don't want to share my cars because I've just parked them all carefully in the garage for the night' or 'This is my doll and I want to look after her myself, but this is your doll and you can look after him'.

Calm statements and sensibly reasoned arguments like this should be respected and children encouraged to make and accept them, provided that they are not over-used. Children may have a few special possessions and some games that may not be disturbed, but they should not be allowed to prevent others from playing by speaking in this way about every toy or game.

Three years to three and a half years

Figure 7.3 Rhythmic physical activities can help children to develop regular and fluent movements and speech.

If children feel very cross because others have unknowingly taken what they wanted or done what they were about to do, they should be supported in saying 'I wanted to do that!' and talking about when they might be able to do it and what they might do now instead.

> Evan, aged three years and four months, and his brother, Leo, aged two years and one month, are playing with a construction kit. Their childminder is helping them to build the walls of a house. Leo is enthusiastic about leaning over to open and close the doors in the walls many times until, inevitably, one falls over. Evan is cross and worried that all the walls will fall if Leo continues to be clumsy and shouts, 'No, you're not being careful enough!'
>
> Evan puts his hands on the other walls to save them and Leo responds by putting his hands on the walls too. The childminder acts quickly to save the game and the relationship by picking up the fallen wall and saying jokingly, 'Oh dear, aren't you funny, Leo? It's just too hard to be careful when you're two and not a big boy yet!'
>
> She immediately continues, 'Let's think of a good idea, Evan. I know, we can put this wall next to Leo, so that he can play with this door, while we build all of the other walls quickly and then stick them together with the roof pieces at the end, so that they can't fall down any more'.
>
> With both boys mollified and playing happily alongside each other again, she gives them each a hug and praises them for the beautiful house they are building together.

Confident adults can influence young children very easily and excited or amused tones of voice are always infectious. Making children laugh and offering reassurance that their problem can be quickly solved, while encouraging them to work together to sort things out, will almost always diffuse arguments and avert potential upsets and ruined games. Children under four do not actually want to disagree with each other, cry, shout or sulk. They would much rather rely on a strong leader to keep the atmosphere and relationships safe and happy, and the more often they experience this attitude, the more easily they will absorb it and go on to use it for themselves.

Explanations and support

Three year olds enjoy real explanations delivered in words that they can understand. Adults must offer reasons for rules and actions, speaking honestly and pointing out facts that the children may not have thought of. Small details appeal to them and allow them to make new connections and progress in understanding.

Instead of simply reminding children not to put puzzle pieces into their mouths, an adult could explain that the picture is made of paper that has been glued onto wood and that paper is spoiled if it becomes wet. If children are interested in the concept, they will enjoy and benefit from experimenting with papers and water. They could try putting pieces of scrap paper, old newspapers and magazines or unwanted packaging into a sink, a water tray or a puddle outside, splashing them with watering cans or leaving them out in the rain to see what happens to them.

If children still struggle to remember not to put things into their mouths by this age, adults need to ensure close supervision and offer consistent advice, such as, 'Always think first – should I put this into my mouth? Probably not. Usually, we should only put food and drinks into our mouths'.

Reminders of what happened to items during games and experiments can be of great help to some children. Adults could take photographs to display as visual clues, remember the exact phrases used at the time to support aural memories and offer the actual items and opportunities to repeat experiments for kinaesthetic learners. Knowing why something is a bad idea communicates the need to avoid doing it much more effectively than simply being told that it is not done.

Between the ages of three and three and a half years, most children will become fully fluent and confident speakers. They will already have very large vocabularies, but be interested in all the new words that they hear, repeating them to practise pronunciations, checking their meanings and using them correcting and appropriately. They will understand information, questions and answers, suggestions, thinking aloud, requests, offers, bargains and fantasies. Imagination and the ability to understand humour will develop, alongside a now well-established enjoyment of dialogue, rhyme and alliteration, provided that they have a rich exposure to language in all its forms and frequent opportunities to use and play with words.

Counting and numbers

Counting songs, rhymes and stories can be used to help children to gradually learn the names and order of numbers and how to count forwards and backwards. They often feel very grown up and gain in confidence and self-esteem

Three years to three and a half years

when they master these, especially since their families will praise them at home and consider this a good thing to have learned and an important milestone.

Figure 7.4 Learning the language of numbers can open up a new world of communication for some children.

Three years to three and a half years

Games and activities using moveable resources, loose parts and attractive pieces can make children want to learn about numbers and go on to develop a deeper understanding of counting, as well as early addition and subtraction.

When children attempt to use more complex words, phrases and sentences but do not manage to get them quite right, adults should simply repeat what the child was trying to say clearly and correctly to provide a model of accurate speech. It is less helpful to directly correct them, to tell them that they were wrong or hard to understand or to make them repeat or change what they were trying to say. If children are treated in one of these ways, they will lose confidence and may stop trying to speak maturely.

Once their mouth muscles and teeth have developed fully and they have heard and practised all of the sounds enough times, children will correct themselves and develop intelligible and fluent speech.

Reading and writing

Some children may begin to recognise written words from this age and all should be encouraged to explore print and text in books, on screens and in the environment around them. Phonic sounds and letter names should both be taught, as many key words and names do not sound the way they are written and phonics or letter names alone can confuse children. A combination of these will be required when learning to decipher words in the early stages of reading and, if all of the knowledge is acquired at the same time and equal importance is attached to each, children will naturally use all of their skills together to make educated guesses and more rapid progress, which will ensure a greater confidence.

They may learn that printed words have meanings and that writing can be understood and used to relay messages or record ideas. Wishing to describe and label the pictures, drawings and marks that they make may lead children to begin to make emergent writing and to ask for support in forming letters and words. They will learn to recognise and read their own names and may begin to write them.

Some children will be ready to take this further and learn to read and write many more words. All children should be encouraged to learn and develop at their own individual paces, with the support of loving carers and dedicated professionals. Just as it is wrong to force a five year old who is not ready to learn to read before basic language skills are well developed, it is wrong to prevent or fail to support a three year old who is capable of becoming a fluent reader and desperately keen to achieve that state.

However, children must be able to speak clearly enough to pronounce and enunciate the words that they will need while learning to read. At the same time, the process of seeing and memorising the shapes and lengths of words and the letters and sounds contained within them enables them to develop a clearer understanding of their speech and vocabulary. Older children and adults will know that a full understanding of an additional language is not acquired unless reading and writing are practised alongside oral activities.

Clear speech

Adults must clearly enunciate new words for children, allowing them to hear each separate sound in order, and check that they are pronouncing the words correctly when they repeat them, as bad habits acquired at this stage are hard to correct later on. Words to be particularly aware of are those that involve three or more sounds and those that have the 'ed' ending after the sound 'ck', such as 'asked'. Children need consistent support and good role models to help them to speak clearly and confidently and to pronounce all of the sounds within words.

A fun way to learn and practise enunciation is to use toy microphones and clipboards with picture clues. Children can be invited to introduce themselves, to talk about a topic that interests them, to tell a story or to pretend to give a report or a weather forecast.

Children who experience speech delay or have difficulties in understanding, processing, forming or expressing speech, whether due to a particular disability or to a combination of factors, are likely to become very frustrated. They may fall behind in development or suffer emotional or behavioural difficulties, needing more adult support and becoming clingy, attention-seeking, disruptive, aggressive or isolated.

If parents or carers, at home or in an early years setting, identify that children's speech and communication skills are not developing normally, they should seek advice from specialist professionals and accept medical help or sessions with a speech therapist as soon as is possible. The earlier children begin to receive targeted support, the more likely it is that they will catch up with their peers and go on to achieve their full potential.

Three years to three and a half years

Figure 7.5 Toy microphones can provide children with an incentive to speak clearly and confidently.

It is hard for a three year old who cannot speak clearly or be understood by other children to join in with games and activities. The more articulate children may misunderstand and mistakenly feel that these children are not interested, not ready, or even not nice, and stop trying to include them. If

Three years to three and a half years

they have a stammer, a lisp or tongue tie, jumbled speech, erratic speed or volume when talking or selective mutism, they will need targeted and specific help and support.

Body language

When children struggle with social interactions, due to additional needs or having to learn a new language, adults must intervene to promote communication, whether this is by speaking for and with children at first, by teaching some mimes, gestures and signs to the whole group or by providing some games and shared activities that do not rely on speech and language skills. It is important to remember that there are other ways to communicate. Waving can show pleasure at greeting a familiar person. Smiling and clapping for another child's achievement or holding out a toy to offer or share can indicate friendship. Laughter is a universal language, understood and shared by people all over the world.

Holding hands can make children feel braver when facing a new experience. In a world often dominated by fear of touches being misinterpreted or unwanted, adults must never stop cuddling babies or hugging young children or encouraging them to play physically, hold hands and share appropriate touches when they choose to. All children need cuddles for comfort and reassurance and the language of hugs can continue throughout life.

Children with no vision, hearing or speech disabilities or special needs will always learn to communicate through words, speech and language, using the information that is all around them, however much or little is available. But, if adults wish to give them the best opportunities to develop strong language skills and the confidence to express themselves clearly, they must always be mindful of the examples they set for children to see and hear, and of providing questions and activities to encourage speech development and extend understanding whenever possible.

Letting creativity soar
Three and a half years to four years

Many children grow up within a community and play with the children of family friends from a very young age. They go on to attend toddler groups, activity classes or early years settings with some children that they know, make more friends there and make the transition to their first school alongside familiar faces.

Social confidence

Young children who have been used to playing with others of mixed ages from their first months will have absorbed an innate understanding and tolerance of differences and types of interaction. They will be able to adapt their approaches effortlessly to play with those who are more or less mature than themselves, respecting others as individuals and learning about them, without needing to know their chronological ages. Children without siblings of their own can learn this from cousins or friends, as long as parents or carers are prepared to make appropriate play situations available on a regular basis.

Those children who do not follow this path might take longer to feel comfortable in their new situations and may not always feel able or willing to communicate with their peers or with the new adults immediately. It is important to allow them the time and space that they need to gain confidence and begin to interact with others when they are ready.

Three and a half years to four years

Figure 8.1 Playing within mixed age groups helps children to understand and tolerate differences in maturity.

Shannon, aged four years and two months, comes from a traveller family and has attended several early years settings in different towns during the past year. She has now joined a reception class in a primary school. In the classroom, Shannon plays alone, but watches the other children, many of whom know each other already, and listens to their conversations without joining in.

At playtime, the children go out into the playground. Shannon sees a group of boys and girls who are running and goes to join them. When they slow down, she calls out, 'You can't catch me!' and runs away, looking back to invite them to chase her and laughing with them when they do. A teacher then brings out some footballs and the chasing game naturally ends, as the children begin to kick the balls around in a large circle instead. Shannon joins in enthusiastically.

Some children move around frequently with their families, for a variety of reasons, and need to learn ways of fitting in and making friends quickly in new situations. Running together, chasing each other and kicking balls are inclusive activities that children instinctively understand. These games have little need for speech or rules and can be shared by those who do not yet know each other, those with little confidence and those who do not have a language in common. Copying each other and sharing physical activities are important ways that young children use when developing communication skills.

When children begin to speak more, develop a wider vocabulary and attempt to use longer words and more complex sentences, they may temporarily struggle to produce all of the sounds in the correct sequences, so their speech might become less clear for a while. They may also have so much to say, or be in such a hurry to tell you everything before they forget it, that their speech might become jumbled or they might even develop a stammer or stutter or muddle some sounds completely.

This is a temporary stage that will go away naturally, provided adults give the children time to speak and listen to them with undivided attention, encouraging them to think about what they want to say and then say it calmly. Hurrying children, paying little attention to them, allowing others to distract them, supplying words for them or correcting them impatiently will make matters worse. Setting an example and modelling calm and unhurried but interesting speech is the most constructive and effective way to help children.

Questions and answers

Rising fours have so many questions that they can hardly formulate them all and ask enough in each day. These questions will include 'What?' 'Where?' 'When?' and 'Who?' but will most frequently be 'How?' and 'Why?' They will ask questions because they genuinely want to know the answers and, if they do not quite understand fully the first time they receive an answer, or want to take a little more time to check their understanding, they will ask 'Why?' again and again. However, saying 'Why?' can also become a habit and a way of maintaining an adult's attention at all costs, sometimes to the detriment of their relationship or the needs of other children.

> Twins, Matthew and Gary, aged four years and four months, ask so many 'Why?' questions that their nanny often has to stop them and distract them with something else to think about. One day, she decides to make time to answer every one, to find out how long it will last if not stopped.

Three and a half years to four years

> Between them, they keep up the questions for over an hour and, to their surprise, their nanny sits calmly on the sofa and gives sensible replies to each one. Suddenly, they look at each other, nod and say, 'Oh, all right then' and go off to play. Their nanny is thrilled.

Parents and carers should make an effort to answer children's questions honestly and sensitively, in clear and simple terms, using words and levels of detail that they will understand. It is necessary to use both knowledge of individual children and general experience of children of this age to reply in ways to which they will respond. But it is also acceptable to maintain some control over the endless 'Why?' questions and to decide when the topic has been covered sufficiently for one day. An adult should be prepared to sometimes say firmly to a child, 'That's not really a "why" question. We've talked about it for a long time today. Shall we do something else now and perhaps talk about it again or look it up in a book tomorrow?' If an interesting distraction is then offered, the child will happily stop and move on.

> Angel, aged three years and 11 months, is shopping with her mother in a large department store and they decide to take the lift down from the second floor to the ground level. Angel watches through the glass walls and says, 'We're going down'.
>
> The lift stops at the first floor to let other shoppers in and Angel moves towards the door. Her mother says, 'No, we're not down at the bottom yet'.
>
> Angel queries this, saying that she saw the lift go down. Her mother explains, 'Yes, we are downer than we were, but only halfway. We're not all the way down yet, so we have to go down a bit more'.
>
> Ignoring the possible opinions of the people sharing the lift with them, Angel's mother chooses to offer the explanation in this way because she knows how her daughter thinks and how she can help her to understand. She is confident that, on this occasion, correct speech and grammar is less important than her effective communication and relationship with Angel.

Guiding behaviour and responses

Sometimes it is important that adult carers are prepared to speak for children, so that others are able to understand exactly what they mean or feel. By the age of four, children are still not able to put all of their complicated ideas, thoughts, feelings and questions into words that others can understand. They may also be relying on those around them having the previous knowledge and experience that their families and familiar carers have, and they are unable to recognise the adjustments needed when communicating with strangers or with practitioners in a new setting.

If adults put their children's thoughts into words for them and then go on to extend the thinking by adding thoughts of their own, the children will develop the ability to think aloud and reason verbally. They will begin to ask questions and answer themselves while playing, creating a narrative or a running commentary, or speaking for different characters while engaged in role play or small world play.

Sometimes it may also be necessary to stand up for a child within social situations and explain if too much is being expected of one so young. Scolding a child in front of others can shake the bond of trust built between a parent or primary carer and their child and should be avoided. When three or four year olds deliberately behave badly, they are often communicating that they are uncomfortable within the situation, that they have become too excited, worried, upset or angry to cope, or that physical needs, such as hunger, thirst, temperature or tiredness need to be satisfied quickly.

Rather than ignoring misbehaviour, making excuses for a child or becoming angry, an adult should quickly apologise and excuse them both, remove the child immediately to a place where they can talk privately and return when problems are resolved, feelings calmed and a new approach agreed upon.

When children lose their tempers at home, or their behaviour spirals out of control when they are alone with parents or other primary carers, the adults may feel upset. Their children may appear to be blaming them for events outside their control or contradicting their decisions unexpectedly, when they have worked hard or struggled against the odds to do their best.

At these times the adults must remember that they are still their children's safe haven and that their shoulders must be broad enough to absorb the children's frustrations, tempers, disappointments, worries and upsets because they cannot yet manage them all for themselves. In fact, families and friends continue to offer this service to each other throughout their lives because

Three and a half years to four years

everybody needs the support of others with whom they can fall apart at times and upon whom they can lean when things go wrong.

When dealing with children of any age, parents, carers and teachers should remind themselves frequently that, 'They may take it out on you, but that doesn't mean it's your fault'.

Children aged between three and a half and four years are usually able to speak confidently and enunciate clearly, although there may still be a few infantilisms or mispronounced words and a few more complex words with combinations of sounds that still need practice. Opportunities to hear and imitate adults forming the words and sounds will usually be enough to support the children in gradually correcting their own speech and acquiring a wide-ranging and effective vocabulary.

Adults should seek to continuously increase children's repertoires and general knowledge during the pre-school years, at the same time as developing their maturity and social understanding. They should use clear speech that is detailed but not over-complicated, modelling correct grammar, pronunciation and good manners, but talk naturally to children, sharing thoughts as they occur, relevant past experiences and plans, hopes and ideas for the future.

Figure 8.2 Children can be encouraged to look outside and remember experiences they've shared in the garden.

Three and a half years to four years

Valuable relationships are strengthened when adults are confident enough to spontaneously sing and chant appropriate songs and rhymes during normal daily life and encourage children to join in. Remembering relevant quotes, events and characters from favourite stories and sharing them at the right moments encourages children to link experiences, make connections and explore creativity. They might also be invited to walk around the home or setting or to look outside in order to recall past shared experiences and add more ideas of their own.

For example, looking through a window into the garden with a child, an adult might spontaneously begin a conversation:

'Do you remember the day we built a den in the garden under the tree?'
'Yes and a squirrel went to play in it when we went inside and had our tea.'
'Yes he did. We watched him through the window, didn't we? But he didn't stay there for long.'
'No, we waved to him and then he ran away.'
'Do you remember how big his tail was?'
'It was long and fluffy and it's called a bushy tail, isn't it?'
'That's right, I love squirrels' soft, bushy tails.'
'So do I.'

> Finlay, aged three years and six months, is offered a snack at a friend's house. She asks him, 'Would you like some of these biscuits?' He happily accepts, but later says, 'These are really called crackers, aren't they?' Anxious not to hurt her feelings or appear rude, he adds, 'Well, they are a sort of biscuits, so you are right, but their name is actually crackers. My Mummy told me that'.

If they have been exposed to good examples and high expectations, children will find it natural to use good manners when asking for what they would like and will be able to describe their needs and intentions in ways that others can understand, being intelligible to strangers as well as to people who know them well. At home or in early years settings, they should be able to care for siblings or friends and be aware of the needs, wishes and feelings of others.

Three and a half years to four years

A teacher or practitioner can provide valuable learning experiences by making arrangements in advance with other adults, to enable children to practise asking politely for what they want and dealing appropriately with the responses they receive. For example, a teacher may take a class of four year olds outside to pick fruit and suggest to the children that they ask the school cooks if they could use the fruit to make puddings for the whole school. Choosing small groups of children in turn, and providing the words they should use to display good manners, will allow all children to learn how to approach less familiar adults appropriately. One child might explain that they have gathered fruit, while another asks if puddings could be made and a third remembers to ask 'Do you have time to help us?'

If the cooks have been privately prepared in advance for the children's requests, they will be able to reply that they do have time to make puddings and thank the children for gathering the fruit. The teacher will then remind the children to say thank you in return. To be adequately prepared for real life, on some occasions children should receive a response of slight postponement or compromise. Cooks may say that, as they didn't know about the fruit in time for today's lunch, they could make it into puddings tomorrow. The children must be helped to understand and agree and then thank the cooks as before.

Between the ages of three and four, children develop an understanding of sharing, taking turns and being fair to everybody. They are ready to learn to negotiate and compromise while playing and to work at building, strengthening and maintaining friendships. They should be encouraged to offer ideas and opinions, but also to listen to and consider the ideas, opinions and responses of their peers. They may advise other children, but will need support to accept that sometimes other decisions will be made by the group.

Children's abilities to work as a group, to consider each other and to learn about teamwork can be enhanced through group activities that all can enjoy together. If adults lead action songs and ring games with enthusiasm, children will learn to join in with others, lead, follow and copy, hold hands and take turns, while they are developing speech and language, understanding, self-confidence, self-awareness and gross and fine motor skills.

In an early years setting, social group or larger family, adults may harness the power of a group and persuade children to work together by asking 'Who wants to do this with me?' or 'Who's good at doing this?' Most children will be carried along by such enthusiasm and happily join in with their peers.

However, this should be avoided in situations that involve one child participating at a time and replaced with 'Jake, could you please help me to do this? Now Max, could you do the next part? Could you help with this, Judy? I think it's Milo's turn now. And then Bella can do the last bit. Everybody else can have a turn to help next time!'

Some children may appear to argue frequently at this age, but this is not always a bad thing, provided they are not defiant or rude. Adults need to encourage verbal reasoning and debate, but help children to use this to resolve problems and issues for themselves, rather than becoming frustrated and upset or blaming others whenever things do not work out as they had planned. They should be supported in talking when they feel cross, until they can ask for help and advice to solve their own problems or feel calmer and move on to a different situation.

Songs, games and stories

Nursery rhymes and simple children's songs, favourite poems and rhyming stories are important at this stage. Three and four year olds need to share these with adults and peers, to develop skills in listening and speech, group cooperation and recognising sounds, word patterns, rhymes and alliteration. These will all be valuable when they join a reception or foundation class and when they begin to learn to read.

Another valuable activity is to play games involving phonetic sounds, such as 'I Spy', or guessing letters and words in books, friezes, posters and jigsaw puzzles. As far as possible, all children should be supported and enabled to learn letter names and sounds securely during their pre-school and reception years, before they move on from the Early Years Foundation Stage.

Singing releases endorphins, which are hormones that make people feel good. It can reduce stress levels and be particularly useful during transitions and other potentially disturbing situations.

When children sing together, they feel that they belong to the group. Sharing traditional songs from different cultures can help children to express their cultural identities and celebrate diversity, but still feel united within their setting. Fitting words to a rhythm and recognising rhymes helps auditory discrimination and confidence in speech and language skills. Singing is particularly helpful to those children who are learning an additional language and to all children when they are learning to read.

Three and a half years to four years

Imagination and creativity are encouraged when children feel confident enough to make up their own songs. Adults need to sing to and with children and to model singing spontaneously and for pleasure at all appropriate times. Recognising that voices are different in pitch, tone, volume and accent, and that many different languages are spoken, should give both children and adults the confidence to express themselves and to sing together.

Most three and four year olds enjoy singing, at least within a group, and also enjoy creating dances or movements inspired by music and songs. Many will be happy to dance or to sing but struggle to do both at the same time, although they may eventually learn to do so if they are provided with opportunities to combine them through action songs and repeating lyrics and choruses. (However, some adults who are talented singers and dancers never manage to confidently do both at the same time!)

Taking turns

Four year olds like to tell adults and siblings about the things that happen or that interest them. Sometimes they can become frustrated and upset because another child tells them first and spoils what they were about to say, or starts a story while they were still working out how to begin, causing an adult to ask questions that they are not yet ready to answer and making them feel muddled. Early years practitioners in settings can help children to develop skills in taking turns to tell parts of a story, by practising this as a game with familiar stories and by inviting them to discuss and speak in turn during a circle time. Parents and home carers can also encourage this among siblings and friends.

Circle times or small group conversations with an interested adult can teach three and four year olds how to take turns to talk and to listen during conversations, enabling them to give and take and to avoid dominating or failing to contribute. Children can learn a great deal from absorbing constructive and rewarding conversations modelled by two adults. At times, another adult may be needed to support the involvement of and non-disruption by a child with special needs within the group.

Early years practitioners and others working professionally with children must model correct, polite and friendly conversations at all times, remembering that the children will always copy them and so they are always 'on stage'! While parents and other family members should offer a more balanced example, including displaying a range of emotions, they should take care when they are in the company of their young children to avoid exhibiting the types of language and behaviour that they do not wish to see imitated.

It may help for adults to gently remind children, 'Now it's Nuala's turn to tell me what happened next' and 'Gareth would like to tell us about the next thing you did'. Children may be supported in saying 'Is it my turn soon?' or 'Now it's your turn and then my turn' to help them to wait and to retain what they want to say in a minute. Small prompts at intervals may also be reassuring for children who are afraid that they will forget everything if they are not allowed to speak immediately.

As they approach the age of four, and are likely to be preparing to go to school within the next year, children will benefit from an organised environment and a more structured schedule than when they were younger. Routines for personal care, such as using the toilet and washing hands or pouring a drink and choosing a snack to eat at the table, should now become familiar and automatic and carried out independently. It may be helpful to talk routines through together and discuss what to do first, next and last.

Special needs

Carers of children with special needs, who need more support with routines, may use a series of signs or pictures to remind them of what to do and the order in which to do it. In early years settings, more able and confident children could be asked to support others by showing them what to do and talking through their actions. Young children will accept alternative methods of communication easily, if they are presented positively, learning key words in other languages, using basic signs or pointing to pictures to help particular friends to understand. All children should be helped to celebrate diversity in this way and to embrace inclusion.

Particular responses or patterns of behaviour, lack of understanding, misunderstanding or incorrect interpretations will indicate to experienced practitioners that children may have specific conditions, such as autistic spectrum disorders including Asperger Syndrome. While some of these children may have few useful verbal communication skills, others will have a highly developed command of language but limited understanding of how to use it in conversation with others. They may interpret every comment literally, as much younger children do, misunderstand social cues and situations and become very anxious when attempting to predict sequences of events.

Three and a half years to four years

Practitioners can help these children to learn more about facial expressions and body language through mime and drama, role play, puppets, songs and stories. Talking about characters and how they feel can encourage them to memorise clues to help them to respond more appropriately to others. It is vital to ensure that their degrees of special educational need are recognised and to seek further help and support from other professionals, in conjunction with the children's parents, when necessary.

Classes and groups

When they reach the age at which their parents choose for them to begin attending a nursery or pre-school, or they join a school reception or foundation class, children need to develop particular skills in order to function happily and successfully within a group. Understanding how to cooperate, knowing when to be quiet and listen to an adult or let others speak and exercising enough self-control to avoid deliberately disrupting stories, games and activities are social, emotional and physical skills that must be learned. It is possible to help and encourage children in this learning by providing fun ways to practise, such as listening games, movement games, taking turns to sing songs or chant rhymes, team-building activities, drama and role play.

Children can try to identify what they hear while listening to a recording of everyday sounds or animal noises, or while standing in the garden, park or playground. Musical statues and other games that require freezing on cue help children to feel comfortable with a lack of movement. Young children seldom sit or stand still for long unless they are very interested in something or they are forced to, as a lack of movement requires the greatest control of the body and they are not yet aware of all of the involuntary movements that they make. Giving them a reason and a desire to be motionless for a very short time allows them to develop the ability to stop and wait calmly until they hear a cue to move again.

Songs and rhymes with repeated lines or question and answer formats can be enjoyed by pairs or groups of children with support from adults. Songs such as: *London's Burning*, *Three Blind Mice*, *Baa Baa Black Sheep* and *Pussy Cat, Pussy Cat, Where Have You Been?* are good ones to begin with. Team games with balls or beanbags, parachute games and passing items around a circle can help a group to bond and learn to cooperate with each other.

Three and a half years to four years

Figure 8.3 Before joining a school class, children should learn how to be quiet when an adult asks them to.

If there are particular concepts that some children in the group are struggling with, they can be encouraged to act them out or to create scenarios with puppets, soft toys or small world figures.

Preparing children for successful interactions in the wider world of school and groups and clubs will also involve giving them the language that they need. Four year olds should be easily able to ask 'May I share?' and 'Can we play together?' in order to seek out new friendships with peers. When speaking to an adult, 'I would like to do that' or 'I would like some help' is more likely to receive a favourable and constructive response than 'I want it' or 'I want you to do it for me'.

> Malcolm, aged four years and five months, likes to discover why things happen and how things work. He enjoys construction toys and builds models in new ways to find out whether they will stay together or balance or move along. He makes scientific connections, such as 'This

> rolls down faster because it's heavier; this gets stuck because it's too big for the inside of the tube; the tarmac is hot because that makes it run out and stick onto the road, then it gets hard when it's cold'. He likes to verbalise his thoughts, to aid his own understanding and memory and to check that his assumptions are correct. He enjoys in-depth conversations with people who are able and willing to explain ideas in detail and to offer interesting information.
>
> In town, his mother buys him a helium balloon in the shape of a favourite character. Malcolm loves holding its string and watching it rise up and follow him, but he also wants to measure and compare it and talk about it: 'This person is quite big, but I'm bigger. But I'm longer and thinner and he's fatter. He's a different shape because he's not a boy'. When they meet an adult friend Malcolm is pleased that she is prepared to discuss his balloon in this way and with a real interest. Where a bland response such as 'That's a lovely balloon' would have patronised and angered him, 'I think that person's about half as big as you, isn't he? But he can fly up in the air, so he can pretend he's taller, and he has such cool glasses!' pleases and stimulates him.

Adults should strive to see things in the way that children see them, in order to hold constructive and stimulating conversations with them. Four year olds are very interested in why things happen and how things work and like to discuss methods and ideas in very logical terms and direct language, often with a great deal of repetition and little regard for correct grammar and word endings.

This method of thinking aloud should be encouraged and supported as it aids their understanding and reasoning skills and helps them to learn to express opinions in a fair and practical way. However, it is worth being aware that, by the age of four, children may often change the subject when they are losing an argument or a discussion is not going in the direction they would prefer.

Reasoning and memory skills

For effective cognitive learning to take place, children must be able to think about their previous experiences and make connections. The sensory information that their brains receive must be absorbed and integrated while they are actively engaged within a stimulating environment and thinking about how things work within the world and in relationships with others. When children have difficulties in absorbing, remembering, understanding, connecting or processing information, they will learn differently from their peers.

When some children's understanding of a situation differs from that of others, they will respond to different stimuli and display different types of behaviour. However, by this age, most children are learning that fitting in with the group feels safe, comfortable and often pleasurable.

If, at times, children find that their responses are significantly different from those of their peers, they may feel that this is negative and to be avoided. While this attitude can give children who are lagging behind in skills considered desirable an incentive to make extra effort to catch up, it may cause others, who are more advanced, to try to hide or deny abilities that they have. Attention-seeking behaviour or unexpected regression in certain areas can often be recognised by experienced practitioners as children communicating their desire to fit in.

Some primary schools use a buddy system that teaches the oldest pupils how they can work with the youngest ones and help them to settle into school life and develop essential skills. These friendships can be beneficial to both the year six pupils and the reception pupils, as they learn about each other and find common interests.

While the older pupils develop patience, listening skills and an understanding of little ones' needs, they can learn to be caring, tolerant and good role models. Although the youngest and least mature children can derive the greatest comfort from their buddies, it is often the more advanced four year olds who find the relationships with their mentors to be most stimulating and who strive to please them and live up to their expectations.

Very able children, who often feel frustrated within their peer groups, may welcome opportunities to work and play harder and at a faster pace, or to attempt new challenges under the guidance of older pupils who will catch and support them and explain how to handle appropriate tasks and common situations. When adults match the pupils carefully and good friendships develop, both age groups can gain a great deal.

It is important to praise all children for understanding and cooperating within the group and for making friends, but also to strive to maintain an enabling environment in which children do not feel the need to be exactly the

Three and a half years to four years

Figure 8.4 Providing opportunities for older and younger pupils to work together can be beneficial to them both.

same as each other. While promoting individuality and diversity, practitioners must treat all children with equal respect and support them all as they find their own ways to excel, encouraging them to recognise and applaud each other's efforts and achievements and to share their triumphs and successes with the right mixture of modesty and pride.

Providing opportunities for children to take messages and deliver them to others is a great boost to memory and communication skills. This may be as simple as, 'Please go and tell Daddy that lunch is ready' or 'Please tell Jane to come to the telephone'. In these cases, the appearance of the correct adult will signify that the message was delivered and understood.

A message could be more complicated, as in 'Could you ask Auntie Jo whether she would like tea or coffee?' or 'Could you go and ask Sue how many children are playing outside?' Children will need to remember and deliver the message, listen to and remember the answer and bring it back to the questioner.

Some messages could require other skills or deductions too. If children are asked to 'Fetch the dog and get him ready to go out', they need to call the

Three and a half years to four years

dog and tell him that it is time to go for a walk, fetch his lead and ball and persuade him to wait by the door. Communicating with the dog will require the special tone of voice and gestures that they have learned gradually through living with him and watching parents and siblings.

If they are asked to 'Find out why the baby is crying and tell her I'll be there in a minute', they must use their knowledge of the baby to check whether she is cross or uncomfortable, frightened or lonely and to try to comfort her and keep her safe until the adult comes to her. They may give her back a lost toy or comforter or play a game to distract her and make her laugh. They may be able to tell the adult that they think her nappy is wet or she is hungry. Having watched previous interactions between the adult and the baby, they will have learned how to communicate with her in a special way. Planning and coping skills are developed and enhanced through thinking about people of all ages, and even animals too, and how to communicate with them effectively.

By the age of four many children will have gained levels of self-confidence and self-regulation that enable them to operate independently in familiar situations and to transfer happily between trusted primary and secondary caregivers. They will be able to cope and interact with others in an early years setting, at the home of a friend or relative or out at a park or playground. They will be aware of their own and others' needs and be in control of their own behaviour, most of the time. But, when something goes wrong, they will need to return immediately to the comfort and security of a parent or carer.

Loving parents are keen to share all the details of their children's lives and naturally want to hear about everything that happens while they are apart. Mummy may ask what happened while they were at Grandma's house. Daddy may want to know what they did at nursery. Grandad may be interested in finding out what the children learned today. A childminder may try to find out more about the children's interests by asking about the games and activities they enjoyed over the weekend. Any of these adults may not realise that they are asking too many questions or expecting detailed answers too quickly.

Children absorb so many impressions and experiences from new environments that they need time to process them all and put them into order, make useful connections and draw their own conclusions before they are ready to talk about them. The task of answering the question 'What did you do today?' can be so overwhelming that they will take refuge in a phrase such as 'I can't remember' or 'I don't know', or just use the word 'Nothing'.

Three and a half years to four years

Although this can be immensely sad and frustrating for their primary carers, who have previously shared every high and low and every moment of the day with the children, it is a phase that will soon pass. Adults must not believe that

Figure 8.5 Children may find it easier to talk about their memories and ideas if they can capture them on paper first.

the children have done nothing, but try to wait patiently and create opportunities for them to talk when they are ready.

Parents and carers may also find that making paper and pens freely available is an effective way of encouraging children to describe their activities and experiences, as they will often draw pictures and designs that represent their thoughts, memories and ideas and then feel inspired to explain or talk about them.

Children will offer information spontaneously, as thoughts occur, memories return and connections are made. Through practice and encouragement, within a calm and relaxed atmosphere, they will learn to organise their thoughts and relate their experiences to adults who are prepared to listen attentively and offer constructive comments to prove their interest. Within a short time the children will be eager to share every detail and bursting to talk about everything they have done as soon as they get home.

The importance of children's close relationships with their families and other primary caregivers is paramount. Adults must work consistently to promote and maintain these, especially among the children of a family. Brothers and sisters do not have to argue or fight with each other and strong leadership from parents, who are always fair and aware of each child's needs and reactions, will ensure that they do not. Good sibling relationships are vital to the happiness and smooth running of the home and family and bring immeasurable rewards that last a lifetime.

Between birth and four years old, children follow an amazing journey, from complete dependence and vulnerability to independence, experience, creativity and resilience. Throughout this time the adults who care for them must inspire, appreciate, develop and support their urge to explore, their sense of fascination and wonder and their intense desire to communicate with the world around them.

Bibliography

Department for Children, Schools and Families (Great Britain) (2008) *The Early Years Foundation Stage: Setting the Standards for Learning, Development and Care for Children from Birth to Five*. Nottingham: DCSF Publications

Department for Education (Great Britain) (2012) *Statutory Framework for the Early Years Foundation Stage: Setting the Standards for Learning, Development and Care for Children from Birth to Five*. London: Early Education

Department for Education and Department of Health (Great Britain) (2014) *Special Educational Needs and Disability (SEND) Code of Practice: 0-25 Years. Statutory Guidance for Organisations Which Work With and Support Children and Young People who have Special Educational Needs or Disabilities*. London: Department for Education

Books

Chalmers, D. (2014) *Speaking and Listening Activities for the Early Years*. Dunstable: Brilliant Publications

Chalmers, D. (2015) *Drama 3–5* (2nd Ed.). Oxon: Routledge

Chalmers, D. (2016) *Creating Communities in Early Years Settings: Supporting Children and Families*. Oxon: Routledge

Sheridan, M. D. (1980) *From Birth to Five Years: Children's Developmental Progress*. (7th Ed.). Windsor: NFER-Nelson

Turecki, S. and Tonner, L. (1995) *The Difficult Child: How to Understand and Cope with your Temperamental 2–6 Year Old*. London: Judy Piatkus

Magazines

Mathieson, K. (2014) 'Positive relationships, behaviour: time to reflect'. *Nursery World* (6th–19th October 2014), p. 32–33

Mathieson, K. (2014) 'Positive relationships, behaviour: in other words'. *Nursery World*. (1st–14th December 2014), p. 32–33

Tassoni, P. (2014) 'Positive relationships, home learning: song times'. *Nursery World*, (20th October–2nd November 2014), p. 32

Tassoni, P. (2014) 'Positive relationships, home learning: singing'. *Nursery World*, (20th October–2nd November 2014), p. 33–34

Tassoni, P. (2015) 'Positive relationships, home learning: a parent's guide to … speech'. *Nursery World*, (23rd March–5th April 2015), p. 28–30

The Communication Trust (2014) Poster: *Cracking The Code! Speech, Language and Communication Needs and the SEND Code of Practice.*

Information online

Information on identifying and helping children who are struggling with speech, language and communication skills. Available from: www.thecommunicationtrust.org.uk/early-years (Last accessed: 9th November 2015).

Index

abuse 87
accidents 69
actions 2; pre-verbal 26, 29; songs 33; to aid speech, understanding or planning 41, 43–4, 56, 74, 84
activities 9; balancing children's needs 23, 41, 66; group 72, 86, 114; non-verbal 102, 104; physical 94
additional needs see special needs
adjectives 31, 87
advice 60, 63, 68, 97
affection 12, 23
alliteration 48, 73, 111
appreciation 77
arguments 96, 111, 116
art see crafts
attachments 22
attention 12, 24, 36, 43, 77

background noise 43, 52
balance 23, 35
battles of wills 62
beats 38, 79–80
behaviour 15, challenging 34, 49–50, 60; examples of 46, 66–7, 92–3; management 87, 107–8; special needs 113, 117
bilinguality 6–7, 13, 30
body language 2, 10, 32–3, 102, 114

bonds 86, 107, 114
books 11, 22–3, 48, 53, 67, 80, 99
bottles 26
boundaries 49
breathing 13

CDs 31, 51
challenges 34–5, 39, 49–50
characters 50–2, 54, 56, 70, 87, 107, 114
chatting 54, 70
chewing 16
choices 40, 49, 57, 94
circle times 75, 112
clapping 7, 11, 14, 24, 44, 102
clues 40, 75, 89, 100, 114
colours 42, 75, 87
comfort 1, 4, 21, 48, 77, 94, 119
comforters 13, 22
comments 31, 42
compromise 110
concepts 48, 75, 87, 97, 115
confusion 48, 76
conjunctions 38
connections 30; experience 74, 97, 109, 115–16; language 37, 60, 66; memory 53, 121
consonants 13, 24, 30, 39
construction 52, 54
control 35, 46

124

Index

conversations 8, 11, 47, 51, 57, 84; with adults 86, 109–12
co-operation 46, 56, 60, 65, 72–4, 111, 114, 116–17
co-ordination 35, 80
copying 1, 7; adults 92–4; language 10, 14, 38; peers 60, 73, 83, 105, 110; signs and actions 44–5, 55
counting 97–9
crafts 52, 87
crawling 14–15, 26
crying 3, 6, 20
cuddles 11, 15, 24–5, 68, 102
cues 31, 74, 91
cultures 13–14, 79, 87, 93
cups 25
curiosity 69

decisions 78, 110
details 96–7, 116, 121
development 60, 63–4
digital media 50, 67
disabilities 41, 77, 90, 100
discipline 40
discomfort 4–5, 31–2
discussion 50, 66, 86, 91, 116
disruption 31–2
distractions 49, 82, 106
diversity 79, 90, 113, 118
dolls 55, 70
drama *see* mime *and* role play
drawing 54, 80, 99, 121
dressing up 52, 72, 87
drinks 25
dummies 13–14
DVDs 50–3

early learning goals 64
early years settings 72, 82, 85, 87, 92–4, 109–10, 112–13
emotions 40, 46, 56, 60, 112
empathy 19–20, 33
entertainment 7, 47
enunciation 23, 33, 43, 100

environment 9, 26, 44, 113, 117, 119
events 26
examples 46, 50, 66, 109, 112
experiences 26, 35, 70, 74, 107, 109, 116, 121
experiments 97
exploration 16, 18, 35, 87
expressions 8; facial 1, 10, 29, 43, 77, 84, 114; of feelings 35, 57, 80
eye contact 3, 18, 39, 48, 83–4
EYFS 64

feeding 4–5
flexibility 85
fluency 51, 57, 97, 99
foundation class *see* schools
friendships 34, 44, 67, 73, 102, 110, 115, 117
frustration 17, 46, expressing 49–50, 60, 64, 100, 107; reducing 15, 34, 39, 43, 61, 69, 111, 117

games 64; co-operative 68, 76, 94, 110, 114; imaginative 56; naming 22; phonetic sound 111; repetitive 16
gestures 11, 14–15, 18, 84, 102
glue ear 43, 57–8
grammar 42–3, 48, 108, 116
groups 28–9
guidance 46, 50, 60, 85

health and safety *see* safety
hearing 11, 57
hearing impairment 43, 57–8

ideas 56–7, 66, 76, 78, 87, 99, 110
ILPs 66
imagination 48, 54, 56, 70, 86, 89, 112
inclusion 33, 113
independence 35, 40, 49–50, 113, 121

125

Index

individual needs 43, 63, 66, 72, 84, 90, 99, 103, 118
infantilisms 38, 57, 108
inflection 18, 38, 42–3, 51, 74, 80
information 31, 62, 66–7, 77, 91, 116–17, 121
instructions 15–16, 30, 41, 43, 62, 68, 81–2, 90, 93–4
intelligibility 71, 99, 109
interactions 1–2, 16, 33, 46, 68, 83–4, 102, 115, 119

jokes 48, 56, 76

key person 25, 32, 66, 86
key words 48, 73, 78, 99, 113
knowledge 86–7, 107

labels 10, 41, 48, 87, 99
language 6–7, 13–14; additional 78–9; delay 60; differences 93; patterns 48; reading 100; social 112–15; sounds 30
laughter 17, 20, 39, 47, 76, 96, 102
letters 99–100
listening 62, 83, 111–14, 121
logic 48, 86

Makaton 44
manners 16, 46, 59, 70, 91–4, 108–10
mark making 99
matching 27, 42, 87
maturity 62, 87, 103
meaning 12, 31, 43, 97, 99
medical conditions 31–2, 100
medication 31–2, 58
meetings 66
memory 22, 27, 40–1, 50, 72, 74–6, 116–18, 121
messages 99, 118–19
mime 15, 43–4, 72, 102, 114
mistakes 36, 39, 42, 63, 71, 101
mobility 16

models 54, 80
mouth 13, 16, 25, 55, 62, 99
movements 8, 31, 72, 114
muscles 13, 99
music 52, 72, 77, 79, 91

names 10–11, 22, 41, 48, 84, 99
negotiation 56, 66, 110
non-verbal 35, 59, 77
nouns 31, 87
numbers 97–9

objects 8–9, 11, 88
observations 64, 66, 87
opinions 57, 78, 110, 116
opportunities 70, 80, 87, 91, 97
outcomes 35, 66
outdoors 80

pace 31, 80, 94, 99
parallel play 59–60
parentese language 4
pauses 18, 80
percussion instruments 79–80
performing 72, 91
personal care 4, 77, 113
phonics 39, 99
photographs 10, 23, 42, 97
phrases 12–13, 16, 18, 30, 36, 38, 43, 97
pictures 10, 22, 42, 73, 99, 113
planning 41
pointing 10, 14, 22
practice 18, 26–7, 31, 36, 91, 99, 108, 114, 121
praise 14, 18, 24, 36, 66, 68–9, 77, 117
predicting 35, 41, 67
preferences 6, 72
problem solving 66, 96, 107, 111
progress 60, 66, 97
projects 66
pronunciation 42–3, 97, 99–100, 108

puppets 87, 114–15

questions 42, 54, 57, 67, 74, 76–7, 80, 105–7, 119

reception class *see* schools
reading 74. 80, 99–100, 111
reasoning 27, 48, 76, 86, 96, 107, 111, 116
reassurance 9, 21
relationships 5; family and carers 16, 20–1, 40, 60–2, 84, 105–6, 109, 121; peers 91, 117; siblings 34, 47, 96
reliability 35
reluctant speech 36–7, 39
repetition 15–16, 31, 41, 43, 48, 70, 91, 116
research 67
resources 85
responses 2, 13; to additional support 66, 113; to instructions 16, 35; to situations 84, 107–10; to speech 31, 35, 39, 42, 115
rewards 12–14, 17, 24, 29–30, 36–7, 76–7, 121
rhymes 31, 33, 38, 48, 52–3, 73, 91, 109, 111, 114
rhythm 2, 6, 31, 38, 73, 77, 79–80
risks 16
role models 46, 80, 100, 117
role play 54–5, 70, 87, 107, 114
routines 26, 41, 48, 53, 81, 113
rules 49, 96

safeguarding 35, 46
safety 16, 35, 46, 49
schools 91, 103–4, 111, 113–15, 117
security 1, 6, 21–2, 26, 41, 48–9, 84, 119
self care *see* independence
self confidence 26, 37, 39, 65, 72, 85, 97, 110
self esteem 72, 97

SENCO 66
SEND 63–4
sentences 12, 18, 30, 36, 38, 43, 48, 57, 105
sense of humour 56, 97
sequences 27, 41
sharing 23, 33–4, 58–9, 68, 76, 92, 94, 110
shuffling 114–15, 20
siblings 45–7; babies 2, 4, 7, 22; balancing needs 23, 76, 96, 121; playing together 33–4, 59–60, 67–8, 89–90, 92, 96; sharing 58, 76; speaking 57
signals 63
signing 43–4
signs 11, 15, 29, 102, 113
silence 5–6, 57, 49
singing 31, 33, 54, 62, 72, 91, 109, 111–12
sitting 9, 14
situations 38; behaviour in 60; common 62; confidence in 103; imaginative 56; understanding 74, 107, 117
skills 16, 64, 85, 110, 114, 117–19
sleep 5–6, 21
small world play 54, 87, 107, 115
smiling 1, 24, 44, 83–4, 102
social skills 14, 16, 40, 57; conversations 86; games 26, 46; new people 83–4; within cultures 59, 92–3, 107
solitary play 72
songs 2, 31, 33, 38, 48, 52–3; adapting and using 62, 109; group 111–12, 114; sounds and beats 80
sorting 27
sounds 6–7, 11–14, 19, 29–30, 37–8, 79–80, 99–100, 111
special needs 34, 44, 77, 102, 113–14
specialist professionals 66, 91, 100, 114

Index

speech 71, 84; developing 10, 13–14, 18, 99–102; increasing skills 105–13; mouth movements 54–5; rhythm 80; social 92
speech therapist 43, 100
stammer 39, 102, 105
stimulation 1, 7–8, 84
stories 38; memories 109; role play 70, 87; speech 33, 48, 52–3, 73, 91, 111–12
structure 26, 48
supervision 46–7, 49, 54, 58, 85, 97
support 35; for adults 50, 63, 108; for children 53, 60, 66, 77, 91–4, 99, 107, 117–18; special needs 113–14
syllables 24

taking turns 112–13; conversation 2, 6, 11, 18, 45; games 16; sharing 92, 94, 110
talking 7, 40, 53, 54–5, 112–13, 121
tantrums 34, 50, 60–2
teachers 110
teamwork 96
teddies 15, 55, 70, 110, 114
teeth 13, 16–17, 25, 99
television 50–3
textures 8, 16, 87, 90
thinking 30, 59, 74, 85–6, 107, 116–17
tolerance 90, 103, 117
tongue 13, 17

touch 3–4, 8, 16, 21, 90, 102
toys 8–9, 11, 53, 70, 86, 94, 102
transitions 103
triplets 19–20
tunes 38
twins 19–20

understanding 11; demonstrating through actions 26, 113, 117; for safety 35; developing through speech 40–1, 56–7, 74, 76, 91, 97, 102, 116; during challenges 50, 69

verbal 36, 39, 56, 107
verbs 31, 87
vision 10
visual impairment 89–91
vocabulary 9, 29, 57, 67, 70, 74, 97, 105, 108; books and stories 22, 33, 48, 100
vocalisations 8, 16–18
volume 57
vowels 13, 24, 30, 39

walking 14–15, 26
waving 11, 14, 102
words 10–12, 18; additional language 78; phrases 29–31; practising 36–8, 67, 92; reading and writing 80, 99–100; sentences 43; stories, rhymes and songs 33, 48, 91, 97, 111
writing 80, 99–100